The Less-Stress Lifestyle

The Less-Stress Lifestyle

Regain control and rediscover happiness

Carl Vernon

HEADLINE

First published in Great Britain in 2017
by HEADLINE PUBLISHING GROUP

Cataloguing in Publication Data is available from the British Library

Trade Paperback ISBN 978 1 4722 4198 6

Editor: Jane Hammett

Typeset in 11/16 pt Cambria by Jouve (UK), Milton Keynes
Printed and bound in Great Britain by Clays Ltd, St Ives PLC

FSC www.fsc.org
MIX
Paper from responsible sources
FSC® C001695

Headline's policy is to use papers that are natural, renewable and recyclable products and made from wood grown in sustainable forests. The logging and manufacturing processes are expected to conform to the environmental regulations of the country of origin.

HEADLINE PUBLISHING GROUP
An Hachette UK Company
Carmelite House
50 Victoria Embankment
London EC4Y 0DZ

www.headline.co.uk
www.hachette.co.uk
www.carlvernon.com

If I could leave you one thing, it would be this book.

Love you lots. Daddy x ☺

Contents

Are you open to a life-changing challenge?

Living a less-stress lifestyle means you're going to have to fight instincts you've developed over many years.

There are concepts in this book that will challenge many people's core beliefs, so you're going to have to create a whole new system – one that will turn your life around and create the lifestyle of your dreams.

I expect everybody at this point to have doubts but, no matter your current situation, you *can* change your life for the better, and I'll be making a huge effort throughout the book to try to convince you it's absolutely possible. Don't allow your natural doubt to convince you it's not. Everything starts with belief, and making positive changes in your lifestyle won't happen unless you believe you can do it.

You are in control of your life and the lifestyle you want, so let's go make it happen!

Carl Vernon

Chapter 1

Why less stress? Why not stress-free?

Life has a lot to offer when you have the time, passion, and energy to live it.

A stress-free life doesn't exist.

Anyway, if it did, can you imagine how dull it would be? On the other hand, though, a life with too much stress is just as unbearable, so the trick lies in getting the balance right.

My dream of freedom started young. As a kid, I used to lie in my bed staring at my Ferrari Testarossa poster, fantasising about being a millionaire and having all the luxuries life could offer. I came from a humble background, so I knew from a young age that life had more to offer, and I had big plans to make it all happen by my early twenties. Stress and anxiety had other ideas, though, and were quick to throw a giant spanner in the works.

In pursuit of my dream to become a millionaire, I left school aged sixteen. Following a successful career in sales, I started my first business when I was twenty-one. I quickly found out that the business world just wasn't for me. Fighting with competitors and motivating unhappy staff was a never-ending battle – the more I fought, the more disillusioned I became with it all.

I felt stuck. What was I going to do? It was always my understanding that, to achieve my dream of a hassle-free life, of freedom and Ferraris, I had to own a business, employ people, and work endless hours – at least, that's what all the successful people were supposedly doing. I did all these things, but none of it felt right. Honestly, I couldn't cope with the stress. Stress was like my kryptonite. Any hint of stress, and I'd be bedbound with endless illnesses. If it weren't tonsillitis attacking me, it would be a constant headache, neck ache, upset stomach, nausea or colds.

Each day I'd walk into the office with a brave smile on my face, but behind that smile was something very different. I'd go home deeply depressed and anxiety-ridden, drink a bottle of wine, and be lucky to get four hours of sleep a night. Every day was a nightmare, and I was far from being myself. I was living a lie. I could try to medicate the problem, but that didn't feel like a viable option. It would have been another way to disguise what was really going on.

After years of living with crippling anxiety and uncontrollable stress, I simply couldn't take any more. The major recession in 2008 hit my recruitment business hard, and although I felt the full force of its impact, it was just the straw that broke the camel's back – I was already mentally unsteady and the recession just tipped me over the edge. 'Breakdown' is a strong term, as I've seen people who have had complete mental breakdowns, but I'd say I was somewhere close.

I was quickly heading down a dangerous path of self-destruction – one I'd find incredibly difficult to turn back from. I knew that my life would have to change dramatically, or else I would have had a full mental breakdown, committed suicide (which I was contemplating), and/or had a heart attack. I can be very stubborn, though, so I wasn't letting my dream of financial and emotional freedom pass me by. I was determined to achieve my dream; I just had to do it in another way. I had to do it in a way that allowed me to be true to myself – a way in which I could comfortably manage my stress and still achieve my goals.

The start of this process was to change my mentality. I had to break free from the sixteen-hour working days I had been putting in and give myself some breathing space. I had to start thinking differently, and view stress in a new way – by understanding that it would always be part of what I do.

With this fresh outlook and different game plan, I quickly grew comfortable with the fact that a stress-free life didn't exist, and therefore the answer wasn't to try and eliminate stress; it was to manage it better. Rather than focus on trying to banish stress, I decided to concentrate on getting the balance right.

What is the right balance?

I've experienced both ends of the stress scale, and neither had much to offer. I've worked sixteen-hour days and run myself into the ground. If you've read my first book, *Anxiety Rebalance*, you'll know I suffered from crippling anxiety for fifteen years. This led to daily panic attacks, social isolation, overwhelming obsessive compulsive disorder (OCD) and bouts of severe depression. It got so bad that I didn't leave my house for months, spending most of my days in my bedroom with the blankets pulled over my head, filled with fear.

To try and compensate for my years of anxiety and mental torture, I've stripped my life of all conceivable stress. I did it by dramatically dropping my working hours, increasing my relaxation time, and consistently saying no to anything that would cause me even a little stress. This turned out to be just as bad! It only led to me being bored to tears and more depressed, wondering where my life was heading.

Now that I'm a little older and a little wiser, I've just about found the right balance – and I feel much better for it! And that's what this book is about: me showing you the things that have helped me accomplish this balance.

I've been where you are now. I've spent years feeling trapped and wishing for something different, convinced there was more to life but not knowing how to get it. I'm still learning, so in this book I won't claim to know all the answers, but I can tell you what has worked for me: things like cutting my working hours (if I wanted to) and choosing exactly how I spend my time (rather than it being dictated by my boss) has led to me changing from a highly anxious and depressed housebound mess to a best-selling author and self-made entrepreneur.

Over the years I've had to deal with all sorts of things – things that have challenged me, caused me huge amounts of stress, and pushed me to my limits. It took me a while to appreciate that if I wanted a lifestyle that wasn't dominated by anxiety and depression, stress is inevitable. There's no point trying to avoid it, and there's no point in me promising myself (or you) a stress-free life – it doesn't exist. I can, however, promise you a challenge that will change your life.

As I mentioned, a stress-free life doesn't exist, but that's OK. In this book you're going to discover why you need stress in your life, why it's not a bad thing, and how to get stress to a point that's manageable for you. This is all part of achieving a *less-stress* lifestyle: if you realise that stress will always be part of life, and don't fight it, but work with it, you'll feel 100% better.

A less-stress lifestyle is doing wonders for me, and I've never felt more in control of my life, my feelings, and my destiny. I have absolutely no doubt that it will do the same for you.

Why I wrote this book

There are a ton of books available on how to be happy, how to reduce stress, and how to manage your time. You can't search on Amazon without seeing them. So, what makes this book different? For me, even though I've found a lot of books on stress and anxiety useful, there has always been something missing. I'd usually finish a book, and although I felt inspired, I also felt as though I couldn't take all the advice I was being given and so I couldn't achieve as much as I had hoped. That's why, in this book, I've made a big effort to provide a 'one-stop' solution for everything you need to achieve freedom and happiness, including the *what* and *how* of everything I know about living a better life, using realistic and tangible methods.

I must make one thing clear: me writing this book doesn't make it easier for you to create a less-stress lifestyle.

I can't do it for you. I say this early on, because I speak to a lot of people who have read a book and expect it to change their life instantly. That's not going to happen unless *you* make it happen, and it's up to you to make it happen through action.

You'll hear me mention action a lot in this book, because it really is the difference between results and failure, change and stagnation. If you asked me what the difference is between my old life (when I was highly anxious, stressed and depressed), and my life today (which is more balanced, so I am more happy and I have more time), I'd say action. I'm now a doer rather than a talker (I'll cover this a lot more throughout the book, especially in the final chapter.) This isn't to say I didn't learn the hard way. It took me about fifteen years to really understand that life had so much more to offer than what I was getting out of it.

Another big reason for me writing this book is to deliver a message: **if I can do it, you can too.**

I've come from nothing, been given nothing, and everything I've ever achieved I've done myself. I've depended on nobody but myself. Here, you won't find an author who raves about all his achievements, only to find out at the end of the book he's been given millions to achieve them. I didn't have rich parents who happily donated their time and money to making my life a success. I didn't graduate with friends who have set up multi-million-dollar tech companies. In fact, I left school at sixteen with no qualifications, with my only guidance coming from my single-parent mum, who was struggling to do her best. The reality is that I went through years of hardship as a kid (including being homeless and spending time in foster care) and have spent most of my life dealing with crippling anxiety.

Am I looking for sympathy, or an extra pat on the back because of these facts? Nope. I have made the choice to offer a better life for my daughter, and not let the past dictate who I am today by becoming one of life's victims. I choose to follow a different path, however difficult and challenging it is.

Our backgrounds don't matter. We're all different, and we can all succeed if we want to. I say this in case you have any doubts, and to reinforce the message: **if I can do it, you can too.**

Principles of a less-stress lifestyle

Another thing I want to make clear now is that I haven't written this book to dictate the type of lifestyle that is right for you and will make you happy. Ultimately, only you know what that is. If it's travelling the world, or living on a remote island, then that's right for you. If it's buying a big house, having lots of kids, and rarely leaving your sanctuary, then that's also right for you. Happiness is a journey, not a destination. It changes as we change. What made me happy in my early twenties is very different to what makes me happy today.

My intention in this book is to open your mind, and help you see things differently. I know first-hand how difficult it is to try something new. I know how challenging it is to change. This book is based on the things that have worked for me and have helped me create a less-stress lifestyle. Whether you decide to keep your day job, start a new venture, or go and live in the Outer Hebrides, I just want you to know that more happiness and less stress is absolutely possible, even by making small, simple changes.

Many things may be going on in your life right now. Issues relating to relationships, work, money, diet, health, family and friends all dictate your levels of stress and happiness. Sometimes, however, making a small change in just one of these areas can make all the difference.

In this book, I will give you the tools that have helped me make the changes I needed to make to achieve the type of lifestyle I live today. I've provided you with answers that will help you dodge the mistakes that I made, which included not appreciating what I had and not knowing what life can really offer. The truth is, life does have a lot to offer, but most of us are too busy pleasing our boss or other people to appreciate it. At the very least, I want to offer you a wake-up call – a reminder that life isn't all about work and no play, and the lifestyle of your dreams is absolutely possible.

To help me achieve a less-stress lifestyle, I ask myself five questions before making a decision. The answers to these questions prevent me from making time-wasting mistakes – and, more importantly, help me dodge the things in life that cause me too much negative stress and unhappiness.

- Is it worth my effort?
- How much stress will it cause?
- What return will I get?
- How long will it take?
- Will it make me happy?

If I don't like the answers, I walk away.

Am I lazy, unmotivated, or lacking passion? Am I ready to pack my rucksack, become a hippy, and live off the land? Far from it. I just believe in working smart (and hard, if necessary). I believe that there's no point in working hard if you haven't got the time, energy or passion to enjoy it. Most of all, I believe that more happiness and less stress can lead to a more fulfilling and richer life.

Having paid attention to how I feel on my 'happy' days and my 'I could kill somebody' days, there are only a few differences between them, including:

- how busy I am
- what I'm doing
- what I'm doing it for.

In other words, I've managed to sum up what makes me happy in one sentence:

I'm happy when I'm busy doing things *I* want to do.

It's pretty simple, but I believe the key to a happier life is simplicity. If I've got too many plates spinning at once, I get overstressed and ill. Stripping my life down to the bare essentials has helped my focus, increased my results – and, most importantly, made me happier. I've also found that a lot of my unhappiness has come from boredom and from having to do things I don't want to do. (Going to work in the morning to do an unsatisfying job is one example of this.)

Because most of us don't tolerate stress well, if you're in the wrong job it will continually throw you off-balance. This is a big reason why so many of us are constantly stressed and unhappy – we've all got things going on in our lives we don't handle properly and that have been forced on us. And here's the deal – it's not our fault!

It's just the way we've seen things from birth, so we don't know any better. We continue to do these things because we're more afraid of change than we are of staying in our 'safe', familiar life. I hope that this book will give you the confidence to know that change isn't a bad thing, and we should embrace it rather than be scared of it.

Choosing your lifestyle

I started the book by asking if you were up for a challenge for a reason. You're going to have to work against your nature a little here, because the pursuit of a different lifestyle is hard at times. Achieving a less-stress lifestyle means you're going to have to do things differently to the crowd.

When I started to make big changes in my life, such as deciding to spend Fridays with my daughter rather than be chained to a desk, people wondered how I did it. They now want the same thing, but it was a different story when I was on my journey to make it happen. I faced criticism and ridicule from every angle – even the people closest to me wondered why I was wasting my time looking for a new lifestyle. *Stick to your nine-to-five job* (or eight-to-seven, which was more accurate) *and stop wasting your time on things that will never happen*, they said. It wasn't their fault, because (like I said earlier), when we're born into a situation we believe to be the norm it's incredibly difficult not to cast a negative judgement until it becomes reality. At first the Wright brothers were mocked for their vision – and now we all get on a plane as though it's the norm. It takes guts to be a pioneer.

Being comfortable with your lifestyle choice means being faced with raised eyebrows every day. People will wonder why you're starting to do things differently. Even when they don't mean to, they may ridicule you and grab hold of your wings as you try to fly. It's human nature – when we see things that are different to the norm, it intimidates us, and our natural reaction is to reject it. You have to stay strong and stick to the principles in this book. This is the key to your success, which is why this book focuses on not only giving you the practical guidance needed to make the lifestyle changes you want, but also on helping to keep you on the right track by proving that it's possible. I use my experience to prove it – and, like I say, if I can do it, you can too.

> 'Whenever you find yourself on the side of the majority, it is time to pause and reflect.'
>
> — Mark Twain, 'Notebook' (1904)

Criticism and ridicule may come from the people you are closest to (unless they are on the same path as you). When you're reading a book or sitting at your laptop researching your ideas, and they are watching TV, they will wonder why you're wasting your time. If you can ignore this criticism and keep the burning belief in your belly (no matter what your situation is like), you are already streets ahead of everyone who has given up – and believe me, there will be plenty who give up. Look at how many people are obsessed with reality TV! It is easier to switch on the TV than it is to read a book, but unless the programme is educational, where does it get you? We all need to be entertained, and there's nothing wrong with that, but the reason I bring this up is because most of us use TV as a form of escapism too much (including me). A typical day for me was getting home from work, spending the whole evening watching TV, and I'd then go to bed. The cycle continued. My life didn't change.

If we don't break the cycle, how can we expect things to change?

Sometimes, when we're so close to achieving our dreams of freedom and happiness we continue to let doubt in, which is why so many of us end up quitting when we really shouldn't. There is a fine line, though. I wish I had the answer to the question: *When do I quit, and when do I keep going?* When do you start taking Albert Einstein's advice on insanity: 'doing the same thing over and over again and expecting different results'? Unfortunately, we'll never be able to predict the future, so all we can do is keep learning and make sure we're acting on previous mistakes – and not continuing to make the same ones over and over again.

Looking back, I've had lots of ideas that would never have taken off. For example, in my early twenties, I spent £10,000 and three months of my time developing a directory website for anything and everything. I had some good ideas for it, but it would have taken a blue-chip company literally millions of pounds of investment and resources to make it work. I was a lone young buck with no guidance, on a shoestring budget, but at the time, try telling me that it wasn't going to work! Hindsight is a beautiful thing.

I've spent – and lost – loads of time and money on other ideas too. Some I continued longer than others, in the expectation they were going to work, when in reality I should have listened to Albert. I'd dust myself off and try again, but the issue was that I kept trying the same thing over and over again, expecting different results, that never came. I was still stuck in my stress-filled existence with nowhere to go.

If anybody knows exactly when to quit and when to keep going, please get in touch – we could make a fortune! The truth is, nobody knows. Nobody will ever be able to see into the future. Nobody will know if that small step you take today will be the step that changes your life. That's why there is one thing I am sure of:

You should never quit following your dream of freedom and happiness – your less-stress lifestyle.

You only get one life. Don't waste it. You owe it to yourself to get the best out of life by being true to yourself.

I want to help you be the best version of yourself. I want to help you break your current pattern so you can see things differently, and reassure you that you have more options than you believe you have now. I want to show you how to have a less-stress lifestyle.

The journey

From tools to deal with stress, to how you can better manage your time and money, I've listed everything I've learnt, and distilled it into the ten actions you need to take to create your less-stress lifestyle. Information is easier to take in when it's broken down into clear bite-size chunks, which is what I have done here.

I want us to go on a journey together – one that is similar to the one I took. I started with small practical changes that I could implement immediately, and discovered that these small changes weren't so small after all. They quickly led on to bigger changes.

Forget about moving the mountain for now; instead, just keep chipping away at it. The journey requires a little patience, but the long-term rewards are well worth the time and effort. There's no such thing as a 'get rich quick' solution – you usually have to fight for things that are worth having, and these things take time and effort.

Before we look at Action 1, let's begin with appreciating why there is nothing more important than happiness and time (and money).

If you're ready, let's start our journey there.

THE BEGINNING OF YOUR LESS-STRESS LIFESTYLE

Chapter 2

There's nothing more important than happiness and time (and money)

Every moment we live and every experience we have creates a memory, and we draw feelings from these memories. In other words, we're always creating our reality based on what has happened to us in the past. This is an important point to start with, because this is why you'll either live a less-stress lifestyle or be locked away and shackled by negative thoughts.

If you're like most people, you'll be allowing negative thoughts to beat you up throughout the day, from getting up in the morning to trying to get to sleep at night. Stressful thoughts about money, work and family will bounce around in your head constantly.

We're all victims of things that haven't happened yet. We worry about the future, and this constant worry continues to dictate how we feel (by creating memories of how bad our lives are). We fall victim to this negativity, telling ourselves that we're no good and a better life is never going to happen to us. We beat ourselves up every day – and so the cycle continues.

I'm going to provide you with the spanner that you can throw into the cogs so that you can stop the cycle of negativity, giving you the space and time you need to make changes and put an end to living like this. I'm going to show you how you can live a happier, fulfilling life without the interference of stress. You just have to stick with me and be open-minded, because I'm going to challenge a lot of the things you may think are a normal part of everyday life.

Before I hand you this spanner, we need to understand why preserving happiness and time is a must.

Happiness

What's more important than how you feel? Nothing.

When my life was filled with misery, fuelled by constant stress and anxiety, it was a living nightmare. Everything was a chore. I didn't have the energy, passion, or will for anything. I was consumed with fear and used to dread waking up each day. Not wanting to get up and begin a new day is as bad as it gets, and when you wake up with that feeling in the pit of your stomach, the rest of the day tends to continue in the same fashion. I rarely had anything positive to think about, and the memories of previous days only caused more stress, anxiety and misery.

The days, weeks, months and years passed, but I didn't change anything. Looking back, I can understand why. I wasn't stupid; I just didn't know any better. I was stuck in a life I didn't want to live, and didn't see any way out of it. I was more afraid of change than I was of making changes, so I stuck it out, no matter how bad it was.

What makes you happy? It's an important question, because I believe many of us don't know what would *really* make us happy.

If you ask most young people today what would make them happy, a common answer is 'being rich and famous'. They see celebrities living glamorous, carefree lifestyles, and they want a piece of the action. On the face of it, it seems entirely plausible. If you're rich and famous, surely you're happy, right? But maybe not . . .

I once watched a TEDx talk by Robert Waldinger called 'What Makes A Good Life?' in which he describes a study conducted by Harvard University on adult development. The study watched 724 men over 75 years, tracking their lives from a teenager into old age. One of the most significant findings that came out of the study was that **good relationships keep us happy and healthy**. It's nothing to do with money or fame – it's simply that social connection works for people, and loneliness and isolation are highly destructive for us, and can sometimes even be fatal. (The study also showed that, the more socially isolated an individual, the shorter their lifespan.)

This research is a strong indication of why too much stress is so damaging for us. When we're put in a stressful situation it's easy to believe that others are causing us problems, so it makes us think that isolating ourselves from others is the solution to our problems. *If I cut that person out of my life, then everything will be OK*. There is no doubt that you should cut *some* people out of your life (we'll cover toxic people in Chapter 15), but being on your own isn't the solution.

You are your environment. In other words, your environment dictates who you are and the people around you will dictate how you feel. Your friends, family and the people closest to you have a profound impact on your life, whether you appreciate it or not. If your life is full of negative people, such as unhappy work colleagues, it's hard to find happiness yourself. If you surround yourself with positive individuals striving for the same things in life, however, it's easier to achieve it yourself. It pays to pay attention to your environment and the people around you.

This certainly corresponds to my experience. When I think about the highest and lowest points of my life, my social connections and the people around me played a big part in both. The happiest times of my life were when I was sharing my experiences and laughing with other like-minded people. The lowest points were being housebound and socially isolated, stuck in bed, and avoiding people. The longer this cycle continued, the more I dreaded seeing other people, and the more isolated and depressed I became, to the point of becoming suicidal. When all you have is your own company, and you are caught in a spiral of negative and soul-destroying thoughts, the world can seem like a tough place to live in.

When you think about your highest and lowest points, what do they look like? It's highly likely that other people played a part in how you felt. There are over seven billion people on Earth. Humans are social creatures, social interaction is inevitable, and people will always play a part in your happiness.

I've been on a Tube in London at rush hour, crammed in like a sardine – but this is nothing compared to Japan, where staff use big sticks to squeeze people on rush-hour trains. I think we do well, considering it's such a small world. High-rise flats, traffic jams and overcrowded high streets can make us feel like we're suffocating at times. That's why, since people play such an important role in our happiness, we need to look for the good in things – otherwise the world can quickly turn sour.

If you go out looking for horrible people, you'll find them. If you go out with a smile on your face, you'll get smiles back. The world reflects your feelings back at you, and it's up to you to dictate your happiness. Getting along with yourself and others is something you need to consider every day. We have to work consistently at it – I know I do.

I've emphasised the importance of interacting with others here because of its strong link to our happiness, but there are many other ways to explore happiness. We're all built differently and find happiness in different ways. My aim isn't to dictate what makes you happy, but to open your mind to the things that can make it possible – because whatever your situation, good or bad, calm or desperate, you can achieve it more often than not, just by being more conscious about it.

What are your absolute favourite things to do? Like me, do you love eating out? Do you enjoy watching a thrilling, action-packed movie? How do you feel when you watch your favourite singer or comedian on stage? These are the feelings I'm talking about – the feelings we're aiming to tap into more on a daily basis.

Time

Time is just as important as happiness, because if we haven't got the time to enjoy life, there isn't much point in making an effort to be happy. For example, if you're working eighty-hour weeks without spending quality time with your family and friends, there is something seriously wrong with your work–life balance.

It's important to keep an eye on the future, but the only thing that is real (in relation to time) is this moment, right now. So, you'd better start enjoying it!

> 'Life is long, if you know how to use it.'
> — Seneca, 'On the Shortness of Life'

Imagine being told you only have a few months to live. How different would the next few months be? What would you choose to do? And what would you stop doing? What would you regret not having done?

I've always wondered why it often takes a life-changing event (like an illness or near miss) to suddenly make us want to live – mainly because I was one of the ones plodding along in an unhappy life without thinking about much more than survival. Why does it take something so drastic to force us into action and want to start living? Again, I wish I had an answer for you, but I don't. If I could answer this, I'd be able to answer the biggest question of all: what is the meaning of life? But, for a number of reasons, I don't want to go there! It's likely we'll never know the answer to these questions. But we are all on a journey. Maybe there is no end destination? OK, we're starting to get deep now! (I promise, this is as philosophical as the book gets!)

If we delve a little deeper into the subject of time, it gets pretty interesting. I've read some fabulous books that talk about time in detail. Albert Einstein, various philosophers, and Morpheus from *The Matrix* all have interesting views about time, including the fact that it doesn't exist. I have an open mind, and find all the theories curious, but the reality remains the same: every time I look in the mirror, I see a slightly older version of myself. If paradise exists, time may not exist there, but we don't live in paradise, we live on planet Earth. And on planet Earth, if you're late for work you get fired! Here, time is precious, and time pressures and deadlines cause stress, making life hard.

I do believe there are elements of time that are an illusion, though, such as being trapped in the routine of working 9–5 (which is now more like working 8–7). Most of us go to work, shuffle a few papers, make a few calls, and tap on our computers for eight hours a day because that's the day that's been set out for us (normally by our employers). And it's a win–win for your employers, especially if you finish your work within a couple of hours, because guess what? They give you more work to do! If you're really unlucky, they'll give you so much work you can't feasibly fit it into eight hours, so you also end up spending your evenings catching up and preparing for the next day.

Having said this, nobody has an advantage when it comes to time. There are always twenty-four hours in the day, and we all have access to every one of them. You'll either waste these hours or use them to your advantage. There is no in-between. I urge you not to get to your deathbed and regret the time that you wasted. The time for change is now!

It's never too late to change, and you can start making a better life – and better memories – right now. It's completely your choice. You can begin taking advantage of time by starting something new today. You can either continue to focus on the negatives and build memories that cause stress, anxiety, fear and inaction, or you can start to build positive memories by focusing on what you want, and taking action to get it.

This book will focus on streamlining your life, with a view to giving you a lot more productive time – time that will lead to a higher level of freedom and happiness, while also allowing you to do more of the things you *want* to do. In other words, it will discuss making time work for you.

Initially, it will look at some small practical changes you can make that will then lead on to some big ones – the *real* life-changers. Remember, it's about progression, not perfection. I'd rather see a small change taking effect and gathering momentum, like a snowball, than see you jump straight into the deep end and splash about, fighting for your life. The big changes took me years to develop, and achieving a less-stress lifestyle will take time and practice. It won't happen overnight, but as long as you're taking action it *will* happen.

(Money)

The good ole green stuff. Some say it's the root of all evil, and some say it makes the world go round. Whatever you believe, you'd better get on board with it, because money will forever be part of your life.

Why is the heading 'money' in brackets?
Good question.

Money should always come after happiness because it's a by-product of happiness. I know this because I spent a long time chasing money, and it never made me happy. When I reversed this – by not chasing money and concentrating on being happy in every aspect of my life – I was a lot happier, and money naturally followed.

Believing that money will make us happy is a big problem for most of us. Although we undeniably need money, we shouldn't chase it. Otherwise, like most other things we chase, it will end up owning us. In my case, it kept me trapped in a highly stressful life working endless hours in a job I didn't enjoy, crippled by misery and uncertainty.

I'm keen for this part to sound not too fluffy, because if I'd read this when I was £50,000 in debt (like I was in my mid-twenties), I would have thought it was a load of tripe. You might think, *It's all well and good for you to say that if you haven't got money worries.* I get that, but this is part of the fear cycle we can become trapped in. (The *fear cycle* is the thought pattern we trap ourselves in. Because we think we need money to make us happy, we chase it, and we constantly worry when we don't have it or we don't have enough of it. This thought pattern, fuelled by fear, continues on a cycle until we break it.) Debt and money worries cause us to chase money continually, and chasing money will never make us happy. This is why it feels like we're constantly chasing our tails, and why it's so hard to break free from debt and money worries.

As well as not chasing money, I've come to realise that having lots of money is overrated. As I said earlier, I grew up wanting to be a millionaire, and didn't grow out of this dream until I was in my late twenties. That was when I had a 'eureka' moment and thought: *Hang on, why am I working all these hours being a slave to work and money, when I could easily have a better lifestyle by restructuring things?*

It's not being a millionaire that counts – it's having a millionaire's lifestyle.

This means a lifestyle of freedom and choice – a less-stress lifestyle.

Being a millionaire means very little. It's just a figure. Of course, it would be extremely nice to have a million in the bank, but do you really need that to be happy? I have found the answer to be no. I've realised that, even when I have a lot less money in the bank, I can be happy and still live the type of lifestyle associated with being a millionaire. In fact, the way I've structured my less-stress lifestyle, I'm probably happier than a lot of millionaires because I don't have anywhere near as much stress. (I've met enough millionaires to know this to be true!)

By doing things backwards (chasing the dream of being a millionaire rather than enjoying life), I was crippling myself, just for the sake of having a million in the bank. When you say it like this, it seems silly to want to be a millionaire, doesn't it? That's why the aim of this book isn't to make you a millionaire; it's to live a millionaire's lifestyle – a less-stress lifestyle.

However, we all need money. We need money to live, eat, clothe ourselves, put a roof over our heads, support our families, and to take part in hobbies. But money doesn't have to own you, and soon I'll discuss how you can break out of the rat race, including how to make money work for you.

ACTION 1:
CHANGE YOUR MINDSET

Chapter 3

Changing your mindset

I'm going to cheat a little here, because I said I'd start off with small changes, but I'm actually going to start with the hardest challenge I'm going to give you, which is to change your mindset. I've always found that if I do the thing I least want to do (or find the most challenging), everything after it is a doddle, so I prefer to get it out of the way first. Once you crack your shift in mindset, you'll find that everything else is a breeze.

For me to help you create a less-stress lifestyle, I have to get you on board with a couple of my discoveries that helped me change my mindset.

Work–life balance

If you work full-time, you'll spend most of your days at work, which means it's also your life. This is one of the main reasons so many of us are unhappy. We look at work as though it's a chore, which is understandable because most jobs are. You're in a very exclusive club if you consistently love your job (and, if you do, you're already way ahead of most people, and therefore you should cherish it).

The trouble with adopting the 'just get through it' attitude towards work is that it's not easy to sustain it for five days out of seven – plus, why would you want to live like that? People change jobs for this reason – we try to keep our interest (and sanity) going as long as possible. We fall into the trap of thinking the grass is greener in another job, so change jobs – then often find that the same thing happens in the new job.

There is, of course, nothing wrong with looking forward to the weekend after a long week at work, but the only reason we do this is because it's all we know. It's what everybody else does, and if you think differently and go against the crowd, you're an outcast. Personally, I prefer to dictate my working hours. If I want to take a break on Tuesday afternoon – or get the urge to work on Sunday – I will. I find I'm much more productive and happy working like this. I know that it's not possible to work like this in many jobs, so it also depends on the type of work you're doing and how flexible you can make it. In other words, if you're a banker and you try to set up a less-stress lifestyle, it won't work. Luckily, though, more and more employers are becoming more agreeable to job shares and working at home, to allow people to work more flexibly. This book isn't about helping you become a banker – or any other profession that ties you down.

This book is about helping you create a less-stress lifestyle . . . working on *your* terms.

The only way to get the work–life balance right is to enjoy what you do, whether it's work-related or personal. Finding the things that will help you achieve this is one of the hardest ongoing challenges you'll face but, like changing your mindset, once you crack it you'll be made for life. My aim is to help you achieve this, and uncover things you might not have explored previously.

By merging your passions in work and life, you'll get the balance you're looking for. Stress won't figure as heavily as it does now, and you will be happier.

Stress can make you ill

Above work, money, or anything else, *the* most important reason for changing your mindset is the fact that stress will make you ill. Your health is everything; without it, you have very little. If you've experienced illness through stress, you'll know exactly what I mean.

I can vouch for how ill stress can make you. Before I sorted my life out by creating a less-stress lifestyle, I was constantly ill. Stress always attacked my throat. One year, when my anxiety was at its height, I contracted tonsillitis six times in as many months. I was prescribed antibiotics on each occasion, but none of them worked effectively to clear up the infection. It wasn't average tonsillitis – where you can still work, with just a croaky voice as the main symptom – I was bedbound with a fever, unable to eat or even move.

If it wasn't tonsillitis attacking me, I'd have a headache (which felt like a tight band around my head), neck ache, and a dull pain in my chest – again, all caused by stress. How do I know stress caused these illnesses? Because since I've begun to live a less-stress lifestyle, I no longer suffer from any of these things. I haven't been ill for some time. If I ever get a scratchy throat or a headache, for example, it is always when I'm stressed, such as when moving house or dealing with a heavy workload.

The way my body handles excessive stress is by getting ill, like most of us – although, as I mentioned, a lot of us don't see it like this. I know I didn't. At the height of my anxiety, if you'd told me my illness was down to stress, I would have ignored you and continued living the same way, because I didn't know any better. This was partly because I didn't want to face up to the fact it might be stress-induced – that would make me weak (I would have thought at the time). It's harsh to think this is ignorance.

People who suffer from ongoing illness often have the same thing in common – high levels of stress. Whether it's caused by a demanding workplace or looking after young children all day, stress makes you ill. The symptoms affect us all in different ways and are very diverse.

I was lucky that the extent of my illnesses has been tonsillitis and headaches. Although they kept me bedbound, they are nothing compared to dealing with a stroke or heart attack. I'll let you do your own research (if you want to), but both of these things are connected to too much stress. That's why it's important not to look at stress as a weakness. Everybody has different tolerance levels to it, and you need to get to know yours. If you're ill a lot, and you know you regularly feel under pressure, it could be down to stress. It's your body's way of telling you that you need to slow down and take a look at your lifestyle and do something about it, before it's too late. I don't want to frighten anybody – but it's true. Stress can be lethal – as lethal as working with hazardous chemicals. But stress isn't always visible. If you work with hazardous chemicals, you'll be provided with suitable clothing to protect you. With stress, there is no protective clothing, and it's up to you to recognise your stress symptoms and do something about them. Do not ignore them!

I sound very critical of stress here, but to set your mind at ease I'd like to reassure you that it isn't all bad, and later we'll explore lots of reasons why. It's all about getting the right balance in your life and using stress to your advantage. This is part of changing your mindset, ready for a less-stress lifestyle.

It's a habit

The life you're living now is based on habit. We all get stuck in our ways, and sometimes believe things are good for us, even when it's obvious they're not (such as feeling stressed and always being ill). We keep doing these things because we don't know any better, or we don't see a way to change.

I can relate to this. There were long periods of my life where I felt I was going through the motions because that's just how things had to be. Working sixteen-hour days with crippling anxiety is a good example. I did it because I didn't feel I had any way out or any other option. Others seemed to get on with it, so I just followed the crowd, even though they were as stressed and unhappy as I was. It's all down to habit.

Depending on how long you've been living the way you have, your brain has been conditioned to think that way is correct – the longer the time, the stronger the conditioning. That's why, if you've been doing something that is causing excessive stress for some time, you'll keep going no matter the damage it's causing, because you'll find the habit harder to break. It's a little like smoking: we know it's bad for us, but once you've been doing it for fifteen years the habit is much harder to break. (I quit smoking after fifteen years and can testify to this!)

'We are what we repeatedly do.'

— Aristotle

Life can very quickly become a monotonous mess thanks to habit and routine. Our brains like routine (it makes us feel safer when we know what's going to happen), making it very easy to fall into a pattern of getting up at the same time every morning, eating the same unhealthy lunch each day, drinking too much coffee, being bored and unchallenged in our lives, and going to bed at the same time every night. Think about what happened to you last week. Could all the days easily merge into one? If they could, you deserve more!

Life becomes very dull when it's too predictable. We need a healthy dash of uncertainty to keep things interesting, and you can't get that if you're doing the same thing day in, day out.

A less-stress lifestyle is about having variety and enough happening in your life to give you the healthy dash of uncertainty you need. Balance comes when you can dictate how many plates you want spinning at one time, giving you more control over your life – and stress levels.

Why?

Have you ever stopped and thought about *why* you do what you do? Probably not for a while – or perhaps not ever. I'd like to get you in the habit of asking yourself why you do things. In fact, take the opportunity to do it right now. Why do you do what you do? Think about why you get out of bed in the morning, why you do your job, and why you're reading this book. You might like some of the answers, but I bet there are plenty you don't like. Maybe questions like these stump you a little. If you answer *I'm not really sure* to these questions, it's a sign that you need to think about your life and where it's going. That's what I want to help you do.

I'm talking about having **purpose** here. You either have direction, or you don't. If you don't have purpose and direction, somebody else will drive the car and choose your destination for you.

I believe excessive anxiety and stress can be prevented by having purpose. If you have purpose and a reason to live, would you ever consider suicide? An extreme example, but I think it's true. To contemplate suicide would mean that you have completely lost your way. When my anxiety was at its worst, I did just that. I didn't know who I was and felt as though I no longer had a purpose. It's the most horrible place on the planet.

Over time and with a lot of willpower, I overcame this belief by asking myself *why* I was doing something. I'm now in the habit of doing this daily. It helps prevent me from plodding along, feeling depressed and doing things

I don't want to do. It helps me to stop following the crowd and doing things for the sake of doing them.

I want you to start thinking about why you're doing what you do – not just today, but every day. You wouldn't get in a car without a destination in mind, so don't do it in life. What direction are you going in, and why are you heading there? What is your purpose?

It's just as important to evaluate our goals and understand our purpose. If one of your goals is to be a millionaire, but that goal is making you ill, why are you doing it? Stop! There is no point in having wealth without good health. I've used this as an example because it's a very common goal – many people want to be rich, and think wealth will mean the end to all their worries. I was this person. I thought I needed to be rich to be happy – nobody told me that the way I was living would kill me, so I kept following the crowd and pushing for my goal in a way that affected my health and happiness immensely. I don't want to let that happen to you.

Get a sticky note and in capitals write **WHY?** on it. Stick it somewhere visible, and let it serve as a reminder that life has more to offer, and that it's too short to continue living an unsatisfactory life without purpose; a life that risks your health and happiness. This is a good starting point on your journey to a less-stress lifestyle.

ACTION 2:
MANAGE AND REDUCE YOUR STRESS

Chapter 4

Managing stress

You now know that stress will always be part of your life. If you're still in denial about this, don't be – it will! That's why the solution isn't to try and get rid of it; the solution is to manage it better.

If you want to live the type of lifestyle you dream of, stress is going to be part of that, whatever you try to do. Fighting against something that you can never win is a poor strategy, so let's look at ways you can manage stress better and work with it, not against it.

Build a 'stress wall'

After the major recession in 2008, I hit an all-time low. My business and life collapsed. By this point, I'd already been through about ten years of chronic anxiety I'd been hiding from everybody, so I didn't think things could get any worse. I was wrong.

My ability to cope with stress became non-existent. I'd hear the post hit the floor with a thud, and it would send shivers down my spine. All the post I received was bills from companies chasing me and the money I didn't have. I never opened them. Instead, I opted to throw them in a drawer out of sight and pretend they didn't exist. Everything got on top of me, and it felt like I was carrying a ton of bricks on my back.

Panic attacks were a daily occurrence – that was how my body tried to cope with the constant trauma of stress. At the time, panicking felt like the right way to deal with the situation, but it didn't help move me any further forward or help me solve the problem (the fact that my life was a mess and getting worse). It certainly wasn't doing my blood pressure, or health, any good.

After months of being panic-ridden and housebound, I hit a turning point, and gave myself two options. (1) End the constant mental bombardment of worry by committing suicide, or (2) Get out of bed and do something to change my situation. And, at the time, both options seemed viable. However, I decided on the latter.

At the time, my partner Lisa's mother was suffering from terminal cancer, which was a big reason why I decided to change: I wasn't doing it for me, but for Lisa. How could I be so selfish as to leave my partner like that? I asked myself. She needed my strength and support, and I was giving her the opposite. I decided that, whatever I was going through, I was going to do something about it.

Trying my best to gather myself (and control my panic), I remember standing still for a second, wondering how I was going to manage the situation. With adrenaline pumping through my body and panicky thoughts still racing around in my head, I had to separate my mind from the current situation. The way I achieved it was by building what I call a 'stress wall'.

With thoughts like 'what the hell am I going to do?' and 'how am I ever going to deal with this?' attacking me, I somehow had to stop them from dominating my mind. I needed space to think of a clear plan. By building a stress wall in my mind, that's exactly what I did. I pictured a huge red-brick wall that looked absolutely solid – like you could take a sledgehammer to it and it wouldn't make a scratch. I closed my eyes and pictured my thoughts hitting the wall and bouncing backwards. I concentrated on slowing my breathing and relaxing my tense muscles. My shoulders naturally dropped, and my fists unclenched.

Then images of the unpaid bills entered my mind. Previously, this would have been enough to cause panic. Now, I imagined them hitting the stress wall and bouncing straight back.

Using the stress wall enabled me to gradually regain control. The situation remained tough, but so did I. I took small, consistent actions, like deciding to get out of bed rather than pulling the blanket over my head, which led to much bigger changes. I faced the bills, rather than pretending they didn't exist, and called the companies to set up manageable monthly payments. I showed Lisa that she could rely on me for support.

I could have continued to focus on how bad things were and being stressed. But where would that have got me? I continued to use my stress wall to block thoughts like 'you'll never be able to pay those bills' and 'your life is never going to get better', and instead decided to focus on things I could control – things that were real, and not further problems I'd imagined.

Ultimately, these small changes led to me creating my less-stress lifestyle – a lifestyle I wouldn't have dreamed possible just a short time ago – and I have the stress wall to thank for it.

It's easy to allow a problem to get out of hand and completely stress us out, especially if it appears from nowhere and shocks the life out of us. This is going to put your body through a cocktail of chemical explosions, all linked with our survival instinct. Although we can't do anything about how our bodies naturally deal with stress (including all these stress hormones racing around our bodies), we can manage it better.

Whenever something makes you stress out, build a construction in your mind to contain it or block it.

It could be a wall, a box, or a cage. It may help some people to build an actual box from cardboard or paper, and write *stress box* on the side. Whenever a problem arises, write it down on a piece of paper and pop it in your stress box. This will help take it away from your mind, giving you the opportunity to deal with it.

Problems with stress arise when we feel overwhelmed, and as if we have too much to deal with. When things mount up in our heads, it can feel like a ton of bricks is lying on us. By putting your problems in a box, you're freeing your mind. That's why writing your thoughts and problems down will help, and why keeping a notepad next to your bed is handy – if you're losing sleep because thoughts are racing round your brain, write them down and release your mind.

When I built my stress wall to deal with the debt problem, it gave me the time and space I needed to deal with it. It helped calm me down and realise that the problem could be solved. There is something about putting a wall in front of something – even an imaginary wall – that makes it feel more manageable.

The idea behind the stress wall or stress box isn't to try and get rid of your problems or pretend they aren't there – it's designed to help you manage them better. My debt problem was kept behind my wall while I put things in place to fix it, like speaking to companies to arrange manageable payments and focusing on other practical things I could do. Using my stress wall allowed me to focus on the things that mattered (and things I could do something about), meaning I was still moving forward and getting things done. I didn't allow the 'what ifs' to drag me backwards.

The world of 'what if . . .'

Have you noticed that, the more you focus on your problems, the bigger they seem? Have you also noticed how, when you focus on your problems, they continue to duplicate? It's like when Mogwai from the film *Gremlins* gets wet – problems just keep popping up uncontrollably and end up becoming gremlins!

Although most of these 'gremlins' are made up by us, they surround us, suffocate us, and cause us bags of stress. We end up living on an unrealistic planet – or, as I like to call it, the world of 'what if . . .'.

The world of 'what if . . .' is why most of us are insecure. We worry about what other people think of us, and we worry about our partners going off and finding somebody better. These insecure feelings are built on lies – lies created in the world of 'what if . . .'. If we want less stress, we need to start dealing with facts and reality. Worrying about things that are out of your control – and things that aren't real – is a waste of your valuable time and energy.

Worrying about the 'what ifs' was the cause of my constant negative state of mind. It became a habit to worry about things that didn't exist, and when I wasn't worried, I wondered why – to the point I'd create things to worry about! For me, it became a worse habit than smoking. I craved worry as much as I did nicotine – neither of which were good for me.

Although the worry wasn't any good for me, over many years I'd trained my brain to think it was the right way to live. Daily, I was practising how to be a worrier, and I was getting very good at it! The good news, though, is that we can retrain our brains to know that constant worry isn't the right way to live. To start this process, you have to pay attention to your daily thoughts.

When you pay attention to your daily thoughts, you'll appreciate how much you worry about things that don't actually exist. If you think about the thoughts you have that are related to the future (particularly the negative ones), how many actually come true? If it's all of them, give me a call – your gift of seeing into the future is going to make both of us very successful! The fact is, most of these thoughts, like 'nobody will ever accept me' and 'I'll never be good enough', are just examples of us catastrophising – seeing the worst in ourselves and believing the lies. They simply aren't true – but, in the world of 'what if . . .', made-up worries become a reality and become part of that vicious fear cycle.

It really does pay to focus on the things that count, not on things that don't exist. If a thought doesn't allow you to grow and its only purpose is to worry you, ignore it – move on. We have about 60,000 thoughts a day, so it's inevitable some will be negative. You can't prevent these thoughts entering your head, but it's up to you what they mean – and how you react to them. That is something you have 100% power over.

It's up to you where you want your reality to lie. I suggest you stop living in the world of 'what if . . .' and start living in the real world. Dealing with facts and reality will rapidly decrease your stress. If you're facing a real-life stressful event, use the stress wall and 'sit down' gap to deal with it. Stress and problems are always temporary, and there's nothing you can't deal with.

The 'sit down' gap

When we get angry, we do things we regret later on, don't we? It's the same with stress – if you act on something when you're highly stressed, it probably won't be the best course of action. You need to give yourself the time and space you need to deal with the stressful situation, whatever it might be.

This is why I created what I call the 'sit down' gap. Whenever I'm put in a highly stressful situation, one in which my head is spinning with disorientation, I don't make any sudden or rash decisions. I deliberately sit down and create a 'gap' between the situation and me. This gives me the time and space I need to come up with a rational and sensible decision. If I acted impulsively, nine times out of ten I would do something I'd regret.

When a situation is particularly challenging, I'll also use the stress wall by sitting down and closing my eyes. Everything around me seems to fade into the distance, and I drown out all the noise I can hear. I only resurface when I'm ready – when my head is straight and I feel more in control.

Sitting down is key: it forms part of the relaxation process. When we're standing, we feel as though we need to act, but when we sit down it gives us a better chance of calming our minds and bodies. We feel less rushed when we're sitting down.

Try not to use the excuse that you don't have the time to do this. If you want to learn to deal with your stress better and improve your lifestyle you have to make changes, including dropping the typical excuses we use daily. It may well be that you have a meeting, that you can't talk right now, or that your diary is so full you can't see me until next year. Maybe none of these things can be helped, and you're in demand! There is nothing wrong with this unless you're not dealing with the situation properly. Are you busy because you're avoiding the issue of being stressed, and being busy is the only solution you know? Ultimately, busying yourself with things that cause you stress will only produce further problems for you later down the line. If you want to continue being in demand, you have to manage your stress better. You have to give yourself some 'me' time and breathing space. Otherwise, you risk living a lie (like I did), and therefore putting your health and happiness at risk.

No matter how busy you are, everybody has the time to take just a few minutes to sit down. If you feel uncomfortable closing your eyes in public, take five and go and sit in your car or on the toilet. Do whatever you need to do to create the gap you need to deal with your stress. With time and practice, you'll become a master at dealing with any situation that's thrown in your direction. Combine this with the stress wall, and people will start calling you a Zen master!

Parkinson's law

The Wiki definition of Parkinson's law is: 'work expands to fill the time available for its completion.'

Parkinson's law means that, if you have a deadline, you're more likely to get something done within that deadline. If you don't have a deadline, it's highly likely your task will take ages, or won't get done at all.

I don't know about you, but Parkinson's law is accurate for me. If I don't put a deadline on something, it doesn't feel as important to me as a task that has a deadline, even if it is a crucial task. The only time I've managed to get things done within a timescale I never thought possible is when I've put a deadline on the task. Like the law says, it's almost as though time expands to make it happen. Does time expand? Through some form of magic, perhaps? Or is it that you just bust a gut to get an important task done? Whatever it is, it certainly helps to have a deadline.

It's too easy to get into the habit of procrastinating, and before we know it, we become experts at it. Parkinson's law will help you to stop procrastinating, so you can start practising taking action and completing tasks. Before you know it, you'll be an expert at getting things done.

Stress mounts up when things don't get done. Getting things done is important for obvious reasons. One of the most important reasons is that feeling we have achieved something improves our mood and reduces our stress. We feel good when we get things done, and so we do more. There is no greater feeling than taking action and being a doer.

Even if it's not required, I put a deadline on everything. In Evernote (I'll cover this shortly), I make a list of my tasks/goals, with a deadline for completion. I look at my list regularly, which keeps me organised and on track. Because of this, I rarely miss anything, and because I'm getting things done, I feel much, much better for it.

A task with no deadline is dangerous – 'dangerous' in the sense that it will probably never get done! Put a deadline on everything – a goal, a task, the next time you want something to happen – everything. Things get done if they have deadlines. Start using Parkinson's law to your advantage.

Get more 'good' stress

I now believe there is such a thing as good stress. I know this because all the years I tried to avoid stress (in every form) I got absolutely nowhere, fast! I was so afraid of what anxiety and worry had in store for me that I avoided stress in all its forms. I stayed in my comfort zone, which was usually within the four walls of my home.

I always looked upon stress as the horrible feeling that caused me great unhappiness and discomfort. Although I was right, I was looking at it in the wrong way. It turned out that I needed 'good' stress to get things done. You could also look at it like having a sense of urgency, energy, or even passion – I wouldn't be as passionate about achieving something if it wasn't for 'good' stress.

Stress wasn't bad; it was a positive sign that I was moving in the right direction. It was proof that I was pushing the boundaries of my comfort zone, and therefore challenging myself and changing my life. When there was no form of stress in my life, nothing happened. Sure, I was safely tucked at home, living in my tiny bubble, but life was incredibly dull.

We all have to do things that we're not comfortable doing: going to the dentist, taking a test, or speaking in front of hundreds of people will all cause stress and anxiety. However, rather than seeing stress as a horrible, negative feeling, as something to avoid at all costs, try to see it as positive reinforcement that your life is going in the right direction.

Too many of us allow the 'bad' stress to weigh us down. By 'bad' stress, I mean the type of stress that frazzles your brain and overwhelms you, creating a negative reaction like excessive anxiety and worry. 'Good' stress feels different because, although it's still stress, it's the type of stress that motivates you and helps you achieve your goals. With 'bad' stress, we focus on the wrong things – the problems that don't exist (the world of 'what if . . .'). This gives stress a bad name so we try to avoid it, which makes things worse – because it's unavoidable.

Stress will always be part of everything you do. As stress is inevitable, concentrate on experiencing good stress – the type of stress that makes a difference to your life, and the type of stress that helps you achieve your goals and pushes you forward in life.

Learn to let go

When life is full of stress, it becomes like a fairground ride, full of apprehension and worry. We hold on with white knuckles, doing our best to stay balanced. You need to learn to let go and appreciate that it's OK not to have complete control.

Tension is at the heart of all our problems, and learning techniques for how to reduce it is key to a less-stress lifestyle. Tension might manifest itself as a headache, a lump in the throat, or a tight feeling in the chest.

When I was frequently highly stressed and took the time to concentrate on my body, and how it felt, I was surprised by how tense I was. I noticed how much I frowned. How high my shoulders were lifted. How rigid my head and neck were. How curled up my toes were, and how tightly my fists were clenched. Subconsciously, I was tensing my muscles to counteract the feelings of stress, which only resulted in me being more tense!

If you're not sure how tense you are, next time you're watching television (or doing some other activity that requires little effort), become aware of your muscles in areas that are typically affected by tension, including:

- Your shoulders – are they hunched?
- Your facial muscles – are they tensed?
- Your hands – are they clenched into fists?

When you become aware of how tense you are, you might feel tension across your entire body. Wherever and however you feel it, it should help you to appreciate the constant strain stress is putting on your body, both physically and mentally. You have to learn to let go and relax!

> 'Take rest; a field that has rested gives a bountiful crop.'
>
> — Ovid

Being too busy and feeling overwhelmed causes huge amounts of tension and stress. You have to learn to take time for yourself, so below I've listed some popular relaxation techniques. I recommend you research them in more detail, and try them all. Stick with the ones that work for you.

Deep breathing

When you practise deep breathing, you breathe in slowly and deeply, while expanding your belly, allowing your diaphragm to contract. Breathing in this way sends a message to your brain to calm down and relax, which makes it effective for dealing with stress. It is a simple and versatile technique that can be learned and used immediately.

Progressive muscle relaxation

Progressive muscle relaxation is a very effective technique for releasing tension in your muscles: you tense a muscle for a few seconds and then relax it. For example, try clenching your fist for a few seconds and then letting go, releasing the tension so your hand is as loose as possible. Your hand should feel relaxed after doing this a few times. You can use this technique on any muscle in your body, so if you have a particularly tense area, you can concentrate on that. The typical areas that affect many people include the neck, chest, face and shoulders. If you do this daily, you will condition your muscles to relax much more freely and naturally.

Physical exercise

You need an outlet for your tension so it's not trapped inside you and used to create more stress and negative energy. Physical activity is an effective way to release tension, due to the fact you burn energy and feel like you've accomplished something. Yoga and tai chi are known to improve breathing and relaxation and are therefore good for stress and tension. If you're more of a football or boxing fan, join your local club. The aim is to find a physical activity you enjoy.

Mental exercise

You can channel the release of tension through healthy mental exertion. I can, however, think of a few board games that increase tension rather than reduce it, so if it becomes counterproductive, avoid it! Sitting down to do a crossword is relaxing for some people, and stressful for others. Use your common sense: if it's not helping you reduce your stress, try something else.

Meditation

Although I don't practise meditation, I make sure I find a moment to relax every day, especially if I'm busy and find myself dealing with extra stress. People have told me meditation has helped reduce their stress and anxiety, improved their mood, and been good for their insomnia – so it could do the same for you. Meditation takes time to perfect, but if it's something you would like to explore, you'll find apps and videos on YouTube that will help get you started.

Have a clear-out

It feels very therapeutic to have a good clear-out. The more possessions we have, the more emotional attachment we have to them. This emotional attachment isn't always negative, and you'll probably have possessions that bring you great joy and comfort, like your favourite jumper or chair. At the end of your clear-out, I don't expect you to have an empty home! However, there will be some items you just don't need (or want) any more. A good clear-out can make you feel lighter and clearer. I do it regularly. When I looked at my wardrobe I noticed I tended to wear the same selection of clothing all the time, so I packed up all the clothes I hadn't worn for a year and sent them to a charity shop. eBay is marvellous for raising some extra funds from unwanted stuff. You might be surprised by how much you can raise. Maybe you could put the money you raise towards a trip or course?

A change of scenery

If you're constantly looking at the same four walls, talking to the same people, or doing the same monotonous tasks or job, you're not presenting your brain with the variety and challenge it needs and deserves. Predictability is boring, and boredom leads to unwanted feelings, including feeling trapped, leading to stress and tension. So spice up your life a little. Take a relaxing break, change your scenery, and do something out of the ordinary.

Chapter 5

Can you *really* afford it?

I don't just mean a financial cost here – but also an emotional cost.

As well as possessions, everyone has what I call 'emotional attachments'. An emotional attachment can be related to anything you have a connection with – anything that makes you think and feel (a husband or wife, partner, child, friend, pet or hobby are obvious emotional attachments). A less obvious emotional attachment is debt. For example, if you get a loan of £10,000 to buy a car, you'll have an 'emotional attachment' to that debt until you don't have it any more. That's why I've called this chapter 'Can you *really* afford it?' It's not just the monthly payments you need to worry about – it's how making the payments make you feel, and what it does to your stress levels if you struggle to pay.

Your emotional attachments affect what and how you think. When you go to bed at night and can't sleep because of your racing thoughts, if you get upset, or can't stop your worry, it's because of your emotional attachments. The more negative the emotional attachment, the more you'll feel down and stressed, maybe even depressed. It also works the other way, of course – the more positive the emotional attachment you have, the happier and more positive you're going to be.

No matter what you do or how hard you try, external factors will influence how you feel internally. A conversation with a friend, kissing your partner, going to a great conference, hearing your favourite music, and tasting delicious food – your senses are always working. That's why it's important to look at all your emotional attachments to find ways of making more good ones and limiting the bad ones.

Banish the clutter

Something Tyler Durden said in the film *Fight Club* struck a chord with me: he referred to us having too many possessions when he said the things we own end up owning us. I agree. If you want mental and financial freedom, you have to start getting wise about the things you own, and your future purchases.

As I mentioned on page 65 on having a clear-out, I noticed that I only wore a small percentage of the clothes I own. Whenever I went to my wardrobe to pick my outfit for the day, I'd always choose the same clothes. The other clothes were there, taking up space, and when it was time to move house, they just caused me more work. I didn't spend a lot of money on clothes, and therefore ended up with a wardrobe full of stuff I didn't want to wear. One day I decided to banish the clutter, and I gave away all the clothes I never wore to charity. I felt so much better for it, almost as though a bit of space was freed in my mind.

It felt so good that now I banish clutter in the rest of my life too. If I want some new clothes, for example, I'll deliberately spend more on good quality, and make sure – if I buy something – it's because I want to wear it. It doesn't cost me any more than owning a wardrobe full of cheap clothes, because I'm saving money by not buying stuff I'll never wear.

Clutter, whether it's your clothes or an untidy office, prevents focus – and that's not good, because focus is everything. If you clutter your mind with problems, it makes it much more difficult to solve even one problem. If you want the tools to handle your problems and your stress, first you have to give yourself the space to enable you to do it: you have to declutter your mind and your life.

If you want a less-stress lifestyle, decluttering is a must. Make sure your house is tidy. Clean up your office desk. Buy things you'll know you'll use and won't just take up space. Declutter your brain by writing down your problems and dealing with them one at a time. All of this is going to boost your ability to focus, and when you do that, you'll be 100% more likely to achieve your goals. More importantly, you'll also be happier and less stressed.

Don't wait

Putting things off and delaying things is a big contributing factor to our level of stress. When we delay things and put them off, they sit at the back of our mind, adding to our stress. Like a naughty child sitting at the back of the class, they might not be right in your face, but they're causing a nuisance. The only way to get rid of them is to get things done.

Have you picked up a bill, thought about paying it, then put it back down, only to have to deal with it again later? Until you deal with it, it's caused you stress. It may not be keeping you awake at night, but it's sitting in your subconscious eating away at you. This is just one example – think about all the things you're delaying right now. All these things are weighing you down and causing you unnecessary stress.

The solution: **don't wait.** If something can be dealt with there and then (something that doesn't take longer than ten minutes to do), get it done, right away. Don't wait and don't delay. You will feel much better for it, and you will become much more productive.

If the task does require a little more time and focus, make sure you schedule it. For example, rather than having a to-do list, schedule your tasks on a calendar. (To-do lists hardly ever get done because we don't put a deadline or schedule on the tasks involved, which leads to procrastination and putting things off.) Write them down on a day you know you can complete them. For example, if you don't want to pay your water bill straight away, but know that it's due by the 31st, schedule the bill to be paid on the 30th or 31st. Being organised will decrease your stress because you know things are getting done, even if it isn't straightaway. By scheduling tasks you're not overlooking them, so you won't feel stressed when the final bill comes in the post. In this instance, automating your payment with a direct debit is even better, because you don't have to do anything at all. (We'll look at this in more detail in Action 9.)

I use Microsoft Outlook for work and personal tasks, and schedule in everything that needs doing within the appropriate timescale, putting an alarm on each task. When the task is due it pops up on my phone and computer, and I get it done (avoiding the snooze feature). This helps me stay organised, and I never miss anything essential. Most importantly, it helps reduce my stress.

ACTION 3: REDISCOVER HAPPINESS

Chapter 6

The happiness trick

This short chapter is the most profound in this book. I'm a simple chap, so it took me a while to grasp this, but the principle behind the happiness trick – used correctly – will change your life.

The actual principle behind the happiness trick is very straightforward, but the understanding and practice of it can go as deep as you like. I've designed this chapter to be simple and tangible (which is always my intention). It's also designed to be reread as many times as you like, and I recommend that you *do* read it more than once. When you really nail the happiness trick, it will change your life. You'll know when it's starting to make a difference when you're able to connect the dots between happiness and perception. Let me explain.

Everything we do is about **perception**. Perception means the way in which something is seen, interpreted or understood. I mentioned previously that the way we define happiness isn't necessarily important. All that matters is how we feel. Something can be true or false, right or wrong – it doesn't matter. If you draw happiness from it, it works. It's all about your perception and what you believe to be true.

> 'It's not what you look at that matters, it's what you see.'
>
> — Henry David Thoreau

In a BBC news article, I read that the consumer group Which? swabbed thirty-three keyboards at its London office. Out of those, four were found to be a health risk. One of the keyboards harboured more germs than one of the office toilet seats! However, if I put this dirty keyboard in front of you and asked you if you'd prefer to lick that or a toilet seat, I bet I know which one you would pick – even armed with the information I've just shared. That is the power of perception at work.

Our perception is that keyboards don't pose a risk to our health, whereas toilet seats do. I'm not saying we're in the habit of licking either keyboards or toilet seats but, given the option, most people would choose to lick a keyboard over a toilet seat. Why? Because it's what we believe. It's what we perceive to be real. When we think about a toilet seat we think of bums sitting on them, but when we think of a keyboard, we think of clean hands typing.

Bums = unpleasant thoughts.
Hands = well, they're just hands.

With this *perception*, you will avoid the unpleasant thing and go with the thing you're most comfortable with, even if you have evidence that your perception is wrong. I do it – we all do it.

The thing about perception is that it can be manipulated. Think about it like putting on a pair of special glasses. Every time you wake up in the morning you put these special glasses on, and they allow you to see things the way you want to see them. They allow you to perceive things in any way you want, and you get to decide whether or not something makes you happy. The truth is, you already own these 'special glasses'. They are called your eyes! You have absolute power over how you want to perceive the world, and how happy (or unhappy) something makes you feel.

David Brent, in the British TV comedy series *The Office* said a struggling salesman doesn't turn up on a bicycle – he turns up in a newer car. Although it was said in what I think is one of the best comedies ever made, it's a serious and valid point and sums up perception perfectly. If you're struggling in life, with stress and anxiety for example (like all people do at some point), don't turn up to work looking as if you have the weight of the world on your shoulders – walk into the office with a bigger smile. You won't only surprise your co-workers; you'll also surprise yourself. It's a 'fake it till you make it' mentality and a fabulous trick.

Some say this is a form of magic because it works so well; I say it's common sense. You might say it's easier said than done; I say keep practising.

How to use perception

I want you to imagine that your life is a movie, and you are the star of that movie. Everybody else in your life is also acting. There's no script, no boundaries, and you can ad-lib. Got it? OK, now I want you to answer some questions. Take your time with them, and really think about your answers.

- What would you be like? Even down to your smallest actions and movements.
- How would you act? Are you confident, charming and charismatic?
- What would your life look like? Are you happy, wealthy and successful?

Given a choice, and the option to act, why do we usually choose to act differently when it's about the life we want to live? If you think about it, life is just one big act – it's just that some of us are better at it than others.

I can appreciate that a life built on an act is not much of a life if it has no substance. But a lot of us are unhappy and want more out of life – we just don't know how to get it. Acting is a way, and I'm giving you a solution. The reason I say 'fake it till you make it' is because acting is a temporary solution. Act the part until you *become* the part. There is little point building a life on a lie – a life without substance – where you're not being true to yourself. There is no long-term happiness to be taken from that.

It helps me to remember that life can be changed using acting, particularly when things start to get a little heavy. It offers me immediate relief. There's something about viewing something as an act (or game) that takes the potential sting out of it. In fact, it allows me to have more fun. I suddenly appreciate that things aren't always as serious as I'd thought, no matter the situation. With a game, you know you can move on if you lose. The consequences don't haunt you and keep you awake at night.

In other words: 'fake it till you make it!' And that's my advice for achieving a less-stress lifestyle. It is the hardest acting job you'll find in Hollywood, but the pay and benefits are great.

If I want to be something or achieve something, as well as doing it I start *being* it. It's all about perception. When I want something out of life I act exactly like the person who has what I want would act – and, with a bit of time and practice, I become that person. I answer questions differently. I make better decisions. I'm more assertive. I take more chances. My life completely changes. With this new-found persona, I'm able to be a better version of myself, and as time passes I no longer need to imitate, copy or act.

You'll know when the happiness trick isn't working for you when you're playing a role and still feel miserable. In this case, you're not being true to yourself, and if you're not being true to yourself you'll never be happy. You should look to act in a different way. You can still achieve the same goals, just look to do it differently by being more in line with the core of who you are. In other words, if you're still miserable after adopting the style of your idols, choose a different path. If you have the passion and will to succeed, your goal will always be achievable, no matter the route.

When I was young I wanted to be a millionaire. The path I took to achieve it, the one that most other entrepreneurs take, is building businesses. That wasn't right for me. I had to look for a new way – a new act to make it happen. When I took the route that was more in line with the core of who I am, using the strategies you'll learn in this book, I was much happier for it. And happiness is the goal here. No matter your belief or the goal you've set out to accomplish, you should view being miserable as the wrong route, and take another.

The key to making perception work for you is continually viewing life as a game. I regularly ask myself: am I winning or losing?

So, are *you* winning or losing, and who do you want to be?

Chapter 7

Instantly improve your mood

Humans are naturally very fickle. We like something, and then we don't. Skinny jeans are in, and all of a sudden you hate them. A trend is set and then disappears as quickly as it rose. Good news, though – we can use our fickle nature to our advantage, and change our mood from down in the dumps to elation within a millisecond.

However, good mood doesn't last long, and it doesn't take much of a knock to bring us back down to earth. So, the trick lies in learning how to sustain the good feelings as long as we can. Let's have a look at how to instantly change your mood, but also keep it balanced.

Less is more

Do you know which country has the top educational system in the world?

America?

No.

China?

No.

Drum roll, please . . .

It's Finland!

So what has Finland been doing that we haven't? About forty years ago Finland overhauled and reformed its educational system. The result: it went from being on a par with countries like America to being consistently top in the world (according to Michael Moore in his documentary *Where To Invade Next*).

The biggest revelation is what Finland did to achieve its #1 status. You might be surprised to learn that Finnish pupils spend about four hours a day in the classroom (about half the time that British and American pupils spend), and have *no* homework and *no* exams. Children don't start school until they are seven, and until then they are encouraged to play and be children. All children, students and teachers are allotted a considerable amount of time for 'personal development', which is also included in the curriculum. And they consistently outperform all other students across the world.

There has to be a lesson to learn from this, surely? I believe the lesson is that less is more. I can certainly relate to this. I used to think that a flashy sports car, big house and designer clothes would make me happy. I couldn't have been more wrong. Ultimately, they just added to my unhappiness, because I was not only stressing myself out by working every hour under the sun to buy them, I was constantly chasing the next happiness fix – because these things only ever made me happy for a very short time.

Simplicity often equals happiness. The simpler you can make your life, the happier you'll be. But, again, it's about balance. Would living a very simple lifestyle and living off the land make me happy? No. So that's not the solution for me either. I've found that the solution for me is to look within myself, and be honest with myself about the things that bring me happiness – rather than the things I think will, or that I'm told will.

The thing that makes me most happy is freedom. The type of freedom I'm talking about is the ability to structure my days and life according to how I want to do it – not having it dictated to me by others. This type of freedom outweighs all the material possessions I could buy. Again, there is a balance. For example, I'd prefer to have a nice car than to drive an old banger, so I need to be realistic about how I manage my life to achieve that. It will take time, effort and stress, and I'm willing to invest that – as long as I can still have what makes me happy – freedom.

What is complicating your life right now? If you are like me, and freedom brings you happiness, what can you strip out of your life? Do you recognise you're doing things that you *think* make you happy, but which might not really make you happy? Typical examples of this are chasing money, buying possessions that get you into debt, and one-night stands that have no substance. That's a great place to start if you want to improve your mood instantly.

Music

I had forgotten how powerful music could be until I listened to the soundtrack of the film *Interstellar* by Hans Zimmer. The instant the track 'Mountains' kicked in, I was filled with emotion. It took me back to all the heartstring-pulling, intense moments I had experienced when watching the film. I hit the shuffle button on my phone, and something completely different came on (my taste in music is eclectic). Michael Jackson's 'Don't Stop 'til You Get Enough' began, and right away I wanted to jump up, grab my crotch, and moonwalk. Nobody was around, so I did exactly that. (If you were wondering, yes, I'm a bit of a mover.)

Music is so effective at helping us get in touch with our emotions, and it works both ways – positive and negative. Recently, a deal had just fallen through at work, and I was working from home. At the time my daughter was watching the children's TV programme *Peppa Pig*, which has to be one of the most annoyingly happy-go-lucky programmes to listen to. I felt the desire to throw my phone at the TV (luckily, I held back). The deal falling through wasn't good news, but hearing such jolly characters on TV just fuelled my anger further. After that, every time I heard the *Peppa Pig* theme tune I associated it with bad news. It's the way our brains are wired.

The things we remember the most are the things that cause a strong emotional reaction. For example, if you have an argument with somebody and it fills you with anger, hate and fear, you'll remember it for some time. If *Peppa Pig* was playing in the background during your argument, you'll associate it with the argument, which will bring back all the emotions you felt at the time.

You can reverse this by retraining your brain to associate something you perceive to be negative with something positive. For example, I took my daughter to the theme park, Peppa Pig Land, and (short of putting cotton wool in my ears all day), there was no way for me to avoid the theme tune – it played constantly through large speakers all over the park! That day could have been a nightmare; however, I decided to retrain my brain to associate the music with the joy on my daughter's face. Now, when I hear the *Peppa Pig* theme tune, I have a mental picture of my daughter smiling. Admittedly, I'll probably never be the biggest *Peppa Pig* fan, but the more I can associate things with positivity, the better.

Is there something you associate with bad news? If so, how can you retrain your brain to associate it with something positive? Can you use music to change your mood? If your answer is yes, what music is going to do that for you? Create a playlist today and call it something like 'Happy'. Keep adding to it and refresh it. Go to it whenever you need a boost.

Become addicted to exercise

I'm not going to cover exercise in detail in this book. I have no doubt you've already been preached at about exercise a hundred times already, so I'll do my best to buck the trend. However, there is a reason I've included it in this chapter on improving your mood.

If you enjoy exercise you have a distinct advantage here. But if you're like most of the population, and make every excuse not to get out there and exercise, you need motivation. Exercise can help you to instantly reduce your stress, and there aren't many things you can say that about – which should be all the motivation you need. There are endless benefits to exercise; improved mood is just one of them.

I am by no means a fitness freak. I've never quite achieved the body I want, even though I'm a regular at the gym. I'm not complaining, though. If I didn't go to the gym, I have no doubt I'd be considerably bigger than I am now. Eating out is my favourite pastime. I'm also partial to a glass of wine and a drop of champagne. For me, exercise should be a must. If I allowed myself to get bigger by not exercising, I know I wouldn't feel as healthy as I do now, and when I feel healthy, I feel happier. Who doesn't?

I called this section 'Become addicted to exercise' for a reason. Given a little time (for it to become a habit), exercise has been proven to become addictive. You start to miss it when you don't do it. Your brain will stop making excuses not to work out, and instead you'll dream of hitting the treadmill. You'll also be in a much better place, physically and mentally.

I found it hard work getting into a routine, but as time progressed and I continued to feel and enjoy the benefits of exercise, I did more. My exercise routine quickly became a fixed part of my life. Today, I'm well and truly addicted – and feel so much better for it. I hope I've convinced you to at least give exercise a go (if you don't already), because it will change your life.

Make mornings great

Most people report that mornings are their biggest challenge, both in terms of stress levels and motivation. Getting over not being a 'morning person' is a must if you want to reduce your stress levels and increase your happiness.

Let's start with the most common problem – the snooze button! When you hit the snooze button, you're trying to put a stop on life. Since your first thoughts of the day shape your day, this isn't the best of starts.

There are lots of strategies for beating the snooze button and waking up feeling refreshed and ready to go. If you hit the snooze button every day, I suggest you do some research and find out which one works best for you. The one that is most effective for me is putting my alarm clock (my mobile phone) across the room out of reach, and drinking a cold glass of water as soon as I wake up. The 'alarm across the room' strategy works for obvious reasons – the 'drinking a glass of water' strategy is down to the fact we wake up dehydrated (thanks to sweating through the night), and drinking a glass of water provides you with instant energy and hydration. If it's cold, it's just another technique to wake your senses.

I haven't had to use this technique for a while, as I've found getting up in the morning easier – and I'll tell you why below! I've got into the habit of waking up at least thirty minutes before my daughter, giving me the chance to get my breakfast and shower before she starts to demand things of me! I find this is another good way of reducing stress, because when I wake up feeling tired and rushed, with my daughter shaking my shoulder and telling me to 'wake up, Daddy!' it's not the most relaxing way to start the day.

When we're tired, it's often our body's way of telling us we need water. It's the same with headaches – headaches are caused by dehydration, which is why drinking water throughout the day is essential. When I say 'water', I mean water. Although coffee, tea and fizzy drinks are also liquids, they usually contain lots of other crap (such as caffeine and sugar) that counteracts their potential good qualities, which is why sticking to water is best.

Going back to your first thoughts shaping your day, how can you change your thoughts so they are positive? I say 'change', because most of the thoughts we have when we wake up are far from positive. They are usually related to what we've planned for that day, whether that's completing a spreadsheet or cleaning the house. And I think that has hit the nail on the head: if you *want* to get out of bed in the morning, you have to have something to look forward to – something you want to get out of bed for.

This point was proved further when I was trying to work out how much sleep I needed by reviewing my sleeping pattern over a few weeks. Some days I got eight hours, some days I got five. On the days I got five, I told myself it wasn't enough and, with this belief, I instantly felt drained and tired. The only exception to this was when I was speaking at an event, and was focused on its delivery.

I woke up after five hours of sleep, jumped out of bed, and felt as lively and refreshed as I did when getting eight hours of sleep. This captured my attention, because I then began to notice that, on the days I wasn't focused, it didn't matter how many hours of sleep I got, I still felt tired. That's why I believe we should look more closely at our focus and purpose, rather than on actual hourly figures.

The reason a lot of successful people are early risers is because they love what they do. They have something to get out of bed for. I don't know about you, but I'm the same. If I don't have something to get out of bed for, I struggle to get out of bed – what's the point? I hit the snooze button and avoid the things I'm trying to avoid a little longer. When I have something to look forward to, I jump out of bed like a spring chicken, and snoozing is the last thing on my mind. So having something to look forward to is a definite priority. In fact, I'd say it's the only thing you need to change from being a snoozing addict to an early riser. It's easier said than done; I appreciate that more than most. I have to work hard every day to put things in place that keep me happy and focused, and my finger away from the snooze button.

Stop chasing happiness

Lots of people think that success and achievement are what bring about happiness, but what if you turn this around? What if happiness brings about success and achievement? Isn't that a much healthier way to live your life? We're all running around like headless chickens chasing success, money, fame (or whatever you believe will make you happy), when in reality these things are the primary causes of our anxiety and stress. Buying the car of your dreams might give you a quick fix of happiness, but it's only a matter of time before you go hunting for the next fix. Why? It's the way humans are wired. We have an incessant need to strive for more. We can't change that (and why would we want to?), so we need to work with it.

Rather than continuously chasing happiness, why don't you start being happy, right now? The past and the future are important, but the only thing that's important is *right now*. There's no point in saying you'll be happy tomorrow – it doesn't exist yet. The book *The Power of Now* by Eckhart Tolle explains this concept in depth. The book's message is clear: you're never going to be happy unless you start to appreciate each moment and what you have right now. In other words, it's about being more grateful for what you have, rather than worrying about what you don't have.

Are you saying I should be content and shouldn't strive for more?

No, absolutely not – in fact, the complete opposite. Goals are a healthy part of life, and what give us purpose. What I am saying is that you should regularly evaluate your goals. If your goal is to become a CEO of a large company, and you're killing yourself to get there, is it really worth it? Your health (mental and physical) is everything, so why jeopardise it for the sake of more money and power, when they probably won't make you happy anyway? I used to work long days and run myself into the ground just so I could buy the things I thought would make me happy. Not only did they not make me happy, but the extra pressure I was putting myself under to make enough money to afford them just weren't worth it. It was wrong to think I could work so many hours and still be sane at the end of it. All it did was severely increase my stress and, in the long run, damage my health.

I've met a lot of highly successful and rich people, many of whom are deeply unhappy. They have all the material goods they could want, yet many are deeply depressed and highly anxious – and spend all day wondering why they feel that way. I think I know why – they have been so busy achieving their goals that they have forgotten to be happy. When they finally achieved what they set out to do, and felt that glimmer of happiness, it was too late – they were busy searching for their next 'fix'.

Stress comes as part of everything we do in life – we already know that. Good stress will push us to achieve great things. But when our body and mind are screaming at us, 'Hello, I can't take any more!', why don't we listen? We just keep going and ignore the warning signs until we can no longer ignore them (such as a full-blown mental breakdown). If we stop chasing happiness and appreciate the present moment, maybe we'll give ourselves the chance to listen to our bodies and minds?

There are, of course, some people who become CEOs, and who are very rich, who are very happy. Some people thrive on the pressure and stress these things come with. Are these people superhuman? Maybe. Or maybe they're just being true to themselves and doing what makes them happy.

ACTION 4:
FOCUS

Chapter 8

Focus is everything

You're going to get more of whatever you choose to focus on– it's that simple. If you continue to focus on the stress in your life, whatever the cause, you're going to get more of it. That's why focus is everything, and why you need to work out what you want to focus on.

Next time you're in the car or on a bike, look towards where you want to go, and you'll naturally drift in that direction (make sure you don't hit anything!). Life is very much the same. When you start to focus on what you want, you'll naturally drift towards it. You'll hit some bumps and potholes along the way, but any road worth taking won't have a perfectly smooth surface.

Never underestimate focus. It's the beginning of a journey.

How much more likely are you to achieve a less-stress lifestyle if you focus on it, compared to sticking to the same routine? That's right, 100% more likely! Unless you depend on luck, chance or fate (and I suggest you don't), you have to focus on what it is you want. With a little time and work, these things will become reality.

The law of attraction

You've probably heard of the book *The Secret* by Rhonda Byrne. If not, the principle behind it is the law of attraction, which basically says: 'whatever you focus on, you get more of'. The book has sold over 80 million copies worldwide, and is popular for a very good reason.

We all want to believe there is a secret power governing our happiness, because that would mean that things could just happen to us without us making any effort. It would also mean we don't have to take responsibility for our happiness, and that a bit of positive thinking can change our lives. I read *The Secret* for this exact reason, hoping it might hold the answers to a better life. We all want to get a better life without putting in the effort – that's why the book is so popular. However, positive thinking alone won't take you to the finish line. If you want a happier life and less stress, you have to work at it, not just wish it.

I'm open-minded, and I don't want to burst anybody's bubble, especially if positive thinking was changing lives. But, the reality is, it's not, and we have to work hard at being happy. Don't get me wrong: I'm the first person to say that positive thinking can go a long way. I'd much rather surround myself with positive 'glass half-full' type people. Dreams and aspirations are what drive us to achieve things we never thought possible. But we have to be realistic, and even with all the positive thinking in the world, unless we're also taking action, things don't change.

I look at it as putting yourself in the right place at the right time. In other words, if you don't buy a ticket you won't win the raffle. Buy enough tickets, and the win will come. It might be a big, life-changing win. It might be a small win that helps lead you to other wins. You might get tired of losing and stop buying tickets, resigning yourself to the fact it's just not worth it. Will you ever win when you stop trying? Not without the ticket. You've always got a choice. Buy the ticket and have a go, or save your money and stay as you are. I've had my fair share of losing. I've had times when I've got so fed up I stopped trying. Frankly, my life became dull. There is more excitement to be had when you try, especially when you have fun in the process.

I believe there is a lot of merit in the law of attraction. For any sceptics out there, let's look at the law of attraction principle – 'whatever you focus on you get more of' – in a more practical way. That's just common sense: there's nothing magical or voodoo about that, right? If you focus on getting paid hourly, per shift, per day, or even per year, then you'll get paid in that way. If you focus on a bigger picture – on creating wealth from numerous passive income sources, for example – then that's what you are likely to achieve. Your ambition is part of this process, but if you don't focus on making it happen, it won't. I prefer to make things happen myself, rather than wait for them to happen. When I want something to happen, but don't focus, it rarely does. Again, this is all common sense.

Focusing on what you want (the law of attraction) works. When I believe the world is a horrible place full of horrible people, it delivers exactly that. When I change my mindset and look for the positives in the world and people, people seem to change their attitudes to me and are, in return, more positive.

Ask and you shall receive! (With a bit of work and effort.)

Get to know your 'have tos'

Your 'have tos', as I call them, are the things that live deep inside you, governing what, where, when and how you do things. They define you as a person and are the reason why you achieve your ambitions – or decide not to get out of bed.

Our 'have tos' are driven by our fears, the expectations we put on ourselves, our expectations of others, and our environment. The way we were brought up also plays a part, but before you blame your parents for your stress, be aware that your 'have tos' constantly change. What governed them a few years back might not be what's driving them today.

It's important to get to know your 'have tos' (in other words, get to know yourself), because understanding what drives you, motivates you and gets you out of bed each day will make it easier for you to become happier and less stressed.

Think of 'have tos' like having a deadline. If you knew your exam was on Friday so you had to finish revising by then, how much more likely are you to revise than if you had no deadline? The fear of the consequences (not passing the exam) will drive you to *have to* do it; otherwise, you'll probably fail the exam. If the exam means something to you, you'll revise. If it doesn't, you won't. I realised some time ago that if I didn't really *have* to do something, I wouldn't. My 'have tos' were weak, which allowed stress and anxiety to be a fixed part of my life:

'I'm not getting out of bed today.'
'I'm not going to work.'
'I'm not going to that party.'

What if your life depended on you getting out of bed, going to work, or going to that party? How quickly would things change then? You might wake up tomorrow and the last thing you want to do is get out of bed and go to work, but you do it because you are more afraid of losing your house than you are of going to work. Getting up in the morning and going to work are now your 'have tos'. You can either use them to drive you forward and make the changes you want in your life, or use them to create more stress and anxiety.

Unfortunately, most of us use them to create more stress and anxiety. We don't channel the energy our 'have tos' give us to make things happen. Instead, we allow the stress of *having* to do something eat us up inside and paralyse us with fear, making the decision to stay in bed the easier option. You and I both know it's not the easier option, and you can turn this feeling of fear into action by channelling the power of your 'have tos' correctly.

The way to do it is to have the mentality of getting things done. When you know you *have to* do something, get it done! Don't procrastinate, ponder or delay – just get it done. The more you delay the inevitable, the more painful it will be in the long run.

Sometimes we need a little help, which is why the coaching industry is booming. When we have a goal, whether it's to lose weight or change career, depending on our 'have tos' rarely gets it done, unless there is a specific or desperate need for it. If your 'have tos' were strong enough, you wouldn't be thinking about getting a coach – you'd be getting on with your goal. The reason coaching is effective is because a good coach won't only show you how to do something properly, they will also make you accountable for getting it done. This then becomes one of your 'have tos', making it much more likely to happen. *'I have to do it because Andy, my personal trainer, told me to do it.'* This is an actual quote from me, because I've just started using Andy as a personal fitness coach. I'd been going to the gym for years, doing a similar routine and getting the same results, and in a matter of a few months with Andy I'm already seeing and feeling a big difference.

Use the power of your 'have tos' and make things happen – you'll be much happier for it, and you'll get more done with less stress.

Focus on a goal

If you want to feel less stressed, you need to start focusing on the things you do want, and that means having a goal. A goal will keep your eyes on the prize, which is important, because when you're not focused, your mind will get busy and create problems.

Why do you say focus on a goal, rather than goals?

I like to think I'm an optimistic person with an open mind, and generally I am, but I'm also realistic. I believe you can have too many goals – especially when you're dealing with excessive stress. If you have too many goals, you're less likely to achieve any of them than if you just have one. It's like dealing with problems. If you have a ton of problems to deal with, they're much more likely to get on top of you, so you're less likely to deal properly with any of them. If you pick out one problem at a time and break it down, you're much more likely to deal with it and achieve exactly what you want. That's why I think having one goal is better than having ten.

> 'To do two things at once is to do neither.'
>
> — Publilius Syrus

Having a single goal at a time helps you prioritise and end procrastination. It gives you focus and clarity. Think about the time when you tried to juggle ten tasks at once. You found it hard to prioritise and organise, which meant some of the less rewarding tasks got done, and the big ones were left on the shelf. It's the big ones that will make a difference to your life, and when you focus on the big one you're much more likely to get it done.

You'll also find that your less important tasks will tag along with the big one, and you'll naturally get them done because they'll feel easy compared to the big one. Plus, when you do something small and accomplish it, the next thing will be bigger and better. It's all about momentum, confidence and self-belief – all ingredients that will drive out stress and help you achieve your goal.

As well as getting to know your 'have tos' and having a goal, it's also important to focus on what you want. It will help define your 'have tos', make them stronger, and set you on the right course to achieve your goal. Too many of us focus on what we *don't* want rather than what we *do* want. Remember: what you focus on, you'll get more of. If you focus on what you *don't* want, it's likely you'll get exactly that.

If you're struggling to define what you want, it's worth spending some time thinking about this. Write down all the things you want and put them somewhere you can see them. Here are some of my wants:

- To be a better father by spending more quality time with my family.
- To be financially and mentally free.
- To want to get out of bed every morning.

These should act as a reminder of why you want a different life – a life with more happiness, time and freedom . . . a less-stress lifestyle.

Be specific

Most people's goal, if you ask them, is to be happy – and rightly so. Happiness can lead to pretty much everything you want. But how does simply saying you want to be happy achieve anything? If you highlight the specific actions you could take to achieve happiness, and make these your goal, wouldn't that give you a much greater chance of success?

Your ultimate goal is to achieve a less-stress lifestyle – but, again, that's as vague as saying you want to be happy. Be as specific as you can be about achieving that goal, and ask yourself: 'What can I do today to get me closer to achieving a less-stress lifestyle?'

Touch each daily goal, taste it, smell it. Bring it to life. Make it real. If it helps, put a timescale on your goal. You don't have to, but it may help you. If you're feeling extra-motivated, do it, but if setting a deadline makes you feel more stressed, you're defeating the object by setting it. Work hard and push yourself – just not too hard. You'll know when you're pushing yourself too hard if your goal seems unachievable and you get signs of burning out.

For me, burning out meant feeling tired throughout the entire day. I felt that I had no energy for even the smallest, most trivial task. From getting up in the morning to going to bed at night, everything felt like a chore, and I got short-tempered and agitated easily, usually taking my anger and frustration out on the people closest to me.

Goals can get bigger with time and practice, but they must be achievable to help you build momentum. Listen to your body and your mind. Push yourself when you know you can, and take a rest when you know you need one. Nobody is judging you as much as you're judging yourself. Be realistic – everybody needs a break, even Superman.

Rest assured, as long as you're striving for a goal and you have a specific goal in mind, that goal is much more likely to get done.

ACTION 5:
THINK HEALTHILY AND BOOST YOUR CONFIDENCE

Chapter 9

Think healthily

Healthy mind, healthy body – and vice versa. When we feel good about ourselves we feel happier. And when we feel happier we not only feel less stressed, but we're also able to deal better with the inevitable stress that life throws at us.

The mind and body are entwined, so it's important to look at our lifestyle choices and how we choose to live our lives, because it has a huge impact on our health – and your lifestyle is always your choice. There are, of course, many temptations put in front of us, and most things won't harm us in moderation, but if you're eating and drinking to excess and not exercising to keep fit and healthy, high levels of stress are inevitable.

I've called this chapter 'Think healthily' because it starts with your thoughts before your actions. You are making a decision every day to live your life how you're living it. When you pick up that next piece of cake, you're making a decision to do it. If you can change your thinking, you can change your life. In other words, you have to make a conscious decision to change, otherwise you will keep doing what you've always done, and nothing will change.

I think we can go over the top with what we should and shouldn't do when it comes to being healthier, but here are a few things I do that have helped me stay healthy, sharp, focused, energetic and happier – all factors that contribute to my less-stress lifestyle.

Eat more healthily

There is a strong connection between what we eat and how we feel. If you eat a takeaway every night, you will become one. Your life will be one quick mess, full of rubbish with no substance. If you eat more raw, fresh, organic and natural foods, you will feel more vibrant, energetic and healthy.

Although I don't claim to be a food expert, I've experienced this. To fit in with my hectic work schedule, I used to eat takeaways four or five times a week. I'd grab an unhealthy snack at lunchtime, and forgot what fruit and vegetables were. I was overweight, overstressed and unhappy. When I put a stop to my hectic work schedule and concentrated on me, including improving my diet by eating more healthily, I felt more energetic and regained my zest for life.

It's scary to see what's being added to some 'convenience' food nowadays, especially the amount of sugar many processed foods contain. We're continually duped by 'fat-free' advertising – there might not be any fat in a food item, but instead it's full of sugar, which is just as bad for you! I've heard many nutritional experts talk about how addictive sugar is – comparing it to things as extreme as cocaine. The coca leaf (from the coca plant, which is used to make cocaine) only becomes a drug when it's refined. It's the same with sugar – it becomes bad for you when it's refined and processed.

The key to overcoming this is to be aware what you're eating. Check labels to see how much fat and sugar foods contain, and eat as much raw, unprocessed food as you can. The more processed something is, the worse it is for you. If you think about it, humans weren't built to eat as much processed food as we do. Stone Age people only had access to raw foods. OK, we've evolved, but obesity levels are through the roof because our bodies weren't designed to digest most of the stuff made today. Cakes, chocolate, and all the other 'treaty' foods taste great, but they are far from great for us.

Let's use our common sense and not forget what's important here: your mood and your health. What you eat has an effect on how you feel. When you're stressed and depressed you turn to food – and it's not healthy food. It's usually comfort food – such as food we ate as kids. If we can moderate our intake of this food, we will feel much better.

Start by trying to avoid processed food such as white bread, white sugar and white rice. Limit takeaways and fast food. Avoid foods that are high in sugar, like fizzy drinks and cakes. Eat more raw foods, including organic fruit and vegetables. Just give it a go! You'll never know how good doing these things can make you feel until you try.

Exercise

I won't go into exercise in too much detail because I have no doubt one hundred other people before me have already told you why you should be doing it. So, let's stick with what's important – your mood.

Exercise is as good as anti-depressants for mild depression and low mood – fact.

Need I say any more? I can already see you jumping off the couch heading for the gym! OK, so the book is too good to put down so you'll go to the gym later. Fair enough. But, seriously, if exercise is not already currently part of your daily life, make it so it is. You will feel 100% better.

I exercise most days. It's now a fixed part of my life, and I feel much better than I did when I didn't exercise – when I made every excuse not to do it, including lack of time. When I didn't exercise, I felt tired all the time, and as though everything I did was a chore. It's a horrible way to live.

Exercise doesn't have to mean gyms and Spandex, however. It could be a walk or jog in your local park (even better when the sun is out), gardening, a game of tennis or badminton, or going out for a cycle. I mix my exercise up as much as I can. I'm not a fan of running, so I get my cardio from racket sports like squash and tennis. Try various sports and stick to what you like.

The main thing is trying. If you're not a fan of exercising, force yourself to go and do it. Start small and work your way up. Exercise is proven to become addictive, so after a while, you won't need to convince yourself to go to the gym any more – you'll *want* to do it. Your brain makes it addictive for a reason, and the reason is that it's good for you.

Instantly boost your mood and decrease your stress today – start exercising!

Juice

I don't always get my five a day, so juicing every day makes sure I'm covering all bases. I'm not talking fruit here – I'm talking vegetables. I won't go into the technicalities, but juicing fruit isn't the best way to eat it (it has something to do with the increased sugar when you blitz the fruit). The experts agree that juicing your vegetables is the way to go.

The UK government recommends that you eat at least five portions of fruit and vegetables each day. It's not always easy consuming that amount, so I have a set vegetable juice I drink every day that includes:

- a handful of kale
- a handful of spinach
- a stick of celery
- five medium carrots
- an apple.

It takes me fifteen minutes to make, and seconds to drink. My big tip is to get a decent juicer. Cheaper juicing machines tend to make a mess and don't do a great job. Although juicing fruit isn't ideal (as I mentioned – it's because of the increase in sugar content), I pop an apple in to liven up the flavour. If you find an all-veg juice not sweet enough, add an apple. Experiment and see what you prefer. I've been juicing every day for over five years, and I wouldn't go a day without it. Why? Because I used to be ill daily, and I don't remember the last time I was held back by illness since I've been juicing. I can't prove it's because of juicing, but I'm not going to stop to find out.

Quit smoking

I smoked for fifteen years, and one of the best decisions I ever made was to give up. Not only do I smell much better now, but I can walk upstairs without panting. I also have a fatter wallet and whiter teeth.

I'm not lecturing anybody who smokes, because nicotine is so addictive, but smoking is a really bad habit. When I smoked, I just wanted my next fix. Quitting smoking was one of the hardest things I've ever done, but it was well worth the struggle. You can do it cold turkey, and there are plenty of resources to assist you. If you need help, start with your doctor or a local group.

Some people say that smoking helps to reduce their stress and relaxes them. They are wrong. It's quite the opposite – smoking increases your blood pressure and does all sorts of horrible things to you and your health. Smoking doesn't help you overcome stress, especially in the long term. If you smoke, all you can guarantee is that it's doing you and your health no good.

If you smoke, make a massive effort to quit. It will change your life. You will save a ton of money, improve your mood, feel healthier and, most importantly, significantly increase your chances of creating a less-stress lifestyle.

Limit your alcohol intake

As with all vices, it's about common sense. I like a drink just as much as anybody else, and I'm especially partial to a glass of red wine. Going back to my days of high stress,

I was drinking at least a bottle of wine a night. I don't need to look at government guidelines to know this was too much.

It may be legal, but alcohol is still a drug. In fact, at the risk of sounding like I'm spoiling the party (again), alcohol is a poison (ethanol, the drug used to make alcohol, is a poison). A hangover is a sign that you've had too much to drink and your body is having trouble processing the alcohol.

It can be tempting to use alcohol to try and deal with your stress, and maybe it does offer a sense of relief when you return from a stressful day at work and sit down with a glass of red, but this is a short-term view. A less-stress lifestyle requires you to look at the bigger picture. If you continue to depend on alcohol to relieve your stress you'll never solve it – you'll just keep masking the issue.

Have a social drink or glass of wine with your meal every now and again (if you want to), but if you find yourself using alcohol to deal with stress, you need to look at what else is happening in your life and why you feel the need to drink.

Like I say, it's all about common sense and moderation. Enjoy life using both of these things – that's the less-stress way.

Avoid illegal drugs

I once knew a guy who was addicted to cocaine. He used to wonder why he was so stressed and anxious all the time, and used the drug to compensate for these negative feelings – and so the vicious cycle continued.

Finally, he asked me for help, and my advice was to get help for his drug addiction before he tried to make changes in the rest of his life. He disagreed, and refused to connect his addiction to his stress and anxiety. He is still addicted to cocaine, and his life is rapidly deteriorating. It's incredibly sad, but no matter how much help he is offered he refuses it.

I won't pretend to know what it's like to be addicted to illegal drugs because I've never taken them. If nicotine is anything to go by, I would imagine stopping taking drugs is one of the most difficult things you can do. I know that drug use is prolific in our culture. I know some of you will be using them recreationally. Like alcohol, some of you might be using them to try and control your stress and anxiety. The truth is, they are not doing anything for you, apart from destroying your chances of freedom and long-term happiness.

Illegal drugs are illegal for a reason. They are standing in your way of true freedom and happiness. You won't be able to create a less-stress lifestyle if you're dependent on a substance.

If you need help to beat any addiction (to legal or illegal substances), start by visiting your doctor. There are many people and organisations out there that can help.

Chapter 10

A boost in confidence

So much of what we do, and how well we do it, comes down to what we believe, so before moving on, I want to share a little story with you that I hope will help boost your confidence.

I was speaking at an event some distance from where I lived, and because I had an early start, I stayed in a hotel the night before. After a few hours in my hotel room, it began to get a little cramped, so I went to the bar for a drink. It was a Friday night and relatively busy, but I managed to find a seat at the bar. There were a couple of women sitting at a table close to me, and I noticed a man walk over and start chatting to them. You could tell from their body language they didn't know who he was and, being naturally quite nosey, I decided to shuffle in a little closer to get a better look – and listen.

These women were attractive and well groomed, and the man was physically unattractive. Now, before you criticise me, bear with me. Firstly, I only mention looks because appearance is relevant in the story I'm about to tell – I believe beauty is in the eye of the beholder. Secondly, you shouldn't judge a book by its cover, but we do – that's human nature (and again, part of the point I'm about to make).

I could tell this guy didn't care about what he looked like. He was incredibly charming and charismatic, and had an air of confidence about him. Within thirty seconds he had turned the women's frowns into smiles, and within sixty seconds he was sitting with them, laughing, looking like they were all having the time of their lives. If I wasn't in a happy relationship, I could have been quite jealous at this point!

As the conversation went on (yes, I was still listening – don't judge me!), it looked as though they had all known each other for years. It was all smiles and lots of chat. This guy believed in himself, and this belief oozed out of his pores.

This guy is an excellent example of why so much of what we do and achieve comes down to what we already believe. He *knew* he was attractive, and that's all that mattered. Because of this belief, the women he chatted to also found out how attractive he was.

If chatting someone up in a bar isn't your thing, there are countless other examples. Maybe you've met somebody who you thought would be a certain way, only to be completely surprised when you got chatting to them. What was it about them that won you over? What was it that made them attractive? Confidence and persona, right? Well, the good news is that you can develop these traits, and anybody can boost them with a bit of practice and belief.

You are whoever you *believe* you are.

We are what we *believe* we are

I remember watching a TV shopping channel and having a giggle over what it was selling. The presenter was demonstrating a jacket – a big fluffy thing with pictures of wolves on it. I thought, surely nobody would buy that, but according to the sales figures on the screen they were selling like hot cakes. I thought this was just a ploy to sell more, until a couple of days later I saw a lady sporting one in a supermarket. The thing was hideous, but you could tell she absolutely loved it and thought she looked a million dollars. Who cares what I thought, or what anybody else thought, as long as she felt great?

Again, this is all about perception. You are as beautiful as you *believe* you are. You may well own a piece of clothing that many people think looks hideous, but you love it and think it looks great. As long as you believe that, and you feel good in it, who cares?

I used to care a lot about what people thought of me, including my appearance. I used to let my image stress me out, and if I thought people didn't approve of me, I would feel rejected and depressed. Like most people, I still care about my appearance (enough not to go to the supermarket in my underpants), but with big differences – differences that have boosted my happiness and lessened my stress. If I buy an item of clothing, I'll do so because I like it, not because I think others will. If I go to the gym, it's because I enjoy it, not because I want to impress others with my big biceps. If I cut down on my eating, it's because I want to improve my health, not because a celebrity tells me to.

People will always see you in different ways, and you won't please everybody. Why would you want to, anyway? If you want to make an impression, fine, but don't pretend to be somebody you're not. If you're looking for a meaningful relationship, pretending to be somebody else will only bite you on the bum later in the relationship (if it lasts).

There is nothing wrong with wanting to impress others and improve your appearance – just do it for the right reasons. If somebody can't see your inner beauty, move on. There is someone out there for everybody, and that person is ready and waiting whenever you are ready – whenever you believe in yourself.

Do you believe?

Mr Universe himself, Arnold Schwarzenegger, was literally top of the universe (he won the Mr Universe title aged twenty, and went on to win the Mr Olympia contest seven times). To get there, though, he had to change the way he thought, including what was possible – what he *believed*.

Throughout his life, particularly his early life, pretty much everything was against him. Agents told him he'd never make it as an actor – not only because he was a foreigner in America with a strange accent and a long, unpronounceable name, but because of his size and stature. Compared to other actors, he was huge, and the fact that nobody could pronounce his name should have been enough for him to give up and call it a day – certainly not to go on to become one of the most successful and highly paid actors of all time.

When listening to an audio book of his autobiography, *Total Recall*, the thing that stood out to me was his absolute belief in himself. Even with the odds stacked against him, he didn't stop until he made it happen. He was relentless and tenacious – he believed in himself. He knew from an early age what he wanted to achieve, and nobody was going to stand in his way. You'd have to be from another planet not to know the rest of his story.

Stories like Arnold's have always intrigued me. When I read these types of stories or meet people that have achieved great things, I see the same pattern and the same ingredients that have led to their success. The standout ingredient that comes to the surface time and time again is **belief**.

Henry Ford said: 'Whether you think you can or you think you can't, you're right.' He was right. It's so true. Everything starts with belief. If you start off thinking that something won't work, it won't. If you don't believe you'll win, you probably won't.

No room for doubt

There is a famous coach known as a 'success expert' (an expert in the skill of succeeding). He charges businesses $60,000, and in return, they get a few hours of his time per month – and that's it! He charges this amount, not only because people will pay it and because he can, but because he knows the secret behind the power of charging such a high sum. If he charged, say $200 (a typical amount for a few hours' consultancy), it would not have as much of an impact as $60,000 does.

Imagine you are the person who pays him $60,000. If you had only paid him $200, you might think, *If it doesn't work, I've only lost $200. I can move on and not use this guy again*. Paying someone $60,000 will completely change your mindset. You will feel the advice you are paying for *has* to work; there is no other option. When you start out with this type of mindset, things rarely fail – and this coach knows that. It's so clever; the client already does most of the work.

The only thing that limits us is our belief – the stories we tell ourselves about why we shouldn't do something because it will never work. Tell yourself a better story: a story with a happy ending, a story where you're the hero. It's not that hard to believe; it happens every day. When you believe you're next in line for the goal you want to achieve, there is every possibility that you are. Even if you're not, you're still in the queue, which is improving your chances more and more every day.

There is no point in aiming to achieve a less-stress lifestyle unless you *believe* it's possible. The start of a successful journey begins with belief. You don't need to fall to the ground overcome by belief, but if you're still sceptical about making significant change in your life, you're not ready.

I hope, at this stage, I've done enough to convince you, because no matter what you do from this moment forward, if you don't believe you can succeed, it won't happen.

The start of a less-stress lifestyle begins with belief.

ACTION 6:
MAKE A START . . . AND MAKE A DIFFERENCE

Chapter 11

Making a start

The most important stage of any process is the start, because if you don't start something, it will never happen. You can have the best idea in the world, but if you don't do anything to make it work, it doesn't exist. It's the same with creating a less-stress lifestyle – if you don't start putting things in place to achieve it, it won't happen.

We all make endless excuses for not starting something. *I don't have time today* and *I'll do that tomorrow* are common. Procrastination, self-doubt, fear of rejection and the wrong environment all play their part in why something won't work or won't get done. I recognise how difficult it is to start something, which is why I've highlighted some of the things you can do to get the ball rolling immediately.

Fight for happiness

Making a start requires motivation. So, how do you get motivated? This is the million-dollar question, and the answer will be different for each person. However, there's nothing more worth fighting for than your happiness.

I decided to change my life, because I got fed up with being fed up. Sometimes you have to say enough is enough. You have to stand up and want change enough that it drives you into action and makes you promise yourself that you'll never go back to that horrible stress-filled life again. When you hit this point, you will have a massive surge of motivation. I did. The surge won't last (most surges don't), but it helps you to make a start – and that's all you need.

Stop fighting every day for no reward! Life is a challenge, whatever we end up doing, so you might as well fight for a good cause – your happiness. In other words, start living for yourself and doing what's best for you. Start doing the things that make *you* happy.

What makes you happy? Think about the last time you were really happy. Where were you, and what were you doing? I know I'm happiest when I'm flexible, working on my terms, with nobody telling me what to do, how to do it or when to do it. Like most people, I'm happiest when I'm busy doing things *I* want to do.

Throughout the book, I'd like you to think about what makes you happy. I'd like you to continue to write down things that come to mind, because being able to answer 'what makes you happy?' is the key to starting to lead a better, more fulfilling life with less stress.

Inspired or desperate?

One of the factors that will dictate your stress levels is where you are in life, right now. I've had many times when I've felt stuck, and as if everything I wanted was a step too far away – as if I was chasing something that I'd never reach. It's not easy chasing goals, especially when you think you'll never get there. When you feel like that, it's hard not to give up. Frustration and bitterness kick in. There are only two things that stop me feeling like this and get me out of the mire: **inspiration** and **desperation**.

It's inspiration and desperation that get me off my backside, make me take action, and instantly change my mood.

Inspiration

Real inspiration and results come from real people – individuals who have experienced what it is *you* want to achieve, and who can offer a real-life account of the before and after. When you sort the wheat from the chaff (like the 'get rich quick' schemes and charlatans just after your money), there's a lot of inspirational stuff out there – genuine people who want to make a difference to your life. People like Nick Vujicic.

There is no greater inspiration to me than Nick Vujicic. He is one of the most motivational and inspirational people I have ever watched. He was born without limbs but, despite this, has lived a more fulfilling and happy life than most people. In his position, how easy would it have been to allow frustration and bitterness to take hold, and to want to give up?

Nick says, if it's not possible to get a miracle, become one. He didn't give up – and, whatever your situation, neither should you. No matter how sorry you feel for yourself, you can guarantee there is somebody out there in a much more desperate situation. You owe it to yourself to live the life you want.

You can find out more about Nick on his website: https://www.lifewithoutlimbs.org.

Desperation

When you have a chainsaw behind you running at full pelt and you have nowhere to run but forward, you run forward, fast. In other words, when you're forced to do something (when you *have to* do it), it simply gets done. That's why, when I feel stuck, I deliberately put myself in a desperate situation I know I can't turn back from. I imagine there is a chainsaw behind me. It's surprising how fast the situation changes, and how quickly I take action that leads to change – including a change in mood.

I remember when my business was rapidly declining following the recession in 2008. At the time, I felt that I had no other option but to get a job. I wasn't skilled or trained in anything particular, so I got a job in advertising sales. To cut a long story short, I had a breakdown in my hotel room during the first few weeks of training. It was my body's way of saying it really wasn't the situation I wanted to be in. Anxiety was a big issue for me at the time, too, and my life was a mess. I came to a crossroads. I could either continue on the path of being deeply depressed, living a life I didn't want, or I could salvage the little hope I had and use it to change things and make them better.

I decided on the latter. I quit the job, even though I couldn't really afford to, stripped everything back in my life to the bare essentials, and decided to start again. This was about the same time I started to follow more of my passions, including writing. It all started from a desperate situation. I focused on achieving the lifestyle I wanted, scrapped any chance of a plan B, imagined the chainsaw chasing me at full pelt, and I took action.

It doesn't always work out for the best, but that doesn't bother me any more. What bothers me the most is when I don't take any action at all: when I procrastinate and when nothing gets done. I spent way too many years living like this to be comfortable with it. I would rather live my life taking action knowing that sometimes it won't work, instead of taking the perceived easier option of just letting things happen and hoping for the best.

If procrastination is a problem for you (it is for lots of people), use desperation. Imagine a desperate situation that you can't turn back from. Be prepared for the fact that it won't always work out for the best, but be safe in the knowledge that you're practising how to take action. If you take action enough in your life, good things will come from it – it's guaranteed.

Execution is everything

Motivation and the will to want to change are important, but absolutely useless if you don't execute your plan by taking action. It's like getting into your car and expecting it to drive itself.

Every day, I meet more people who get into their car and expect it to drive itself than people who take the wheel and start driving. The ones who grab the wheel (the executioners) and put their foot down on the pedal are the people who tend to leave everybody else behind, including the 'talkers', who spend all day complaining about why things aren't happening for them, wondering why they are so stressed and miserable. If you're not grabbing the wheel and putting your foot on the pedal, you have nothing to complain about.

If you come up with a great idea, someone is going to copy it – it's the way of the world. So, what's going to be the difference between your work and theirs? The execution of it. That's why execution is everything. It's the only thing that will separate you from the talkers and copiers.

If you have a brilliant, unique idea and want it to come to fruition, so that nobody can steal it from you, you need to carry out your idea – fast. If it is truly unique, about your personal story, for example, you can be safe in the knowledge that nobody will be able to deliver its message as well as you can. Some might try, but people will see past them and go straight back to the genuine source. When you combine your idea with desire and passion, nobody will be able to compete with you.

To be truly happy you have to be true to yourself, and if you are true to yourself, you can guarantee you'll be doing your best work. (We'll cover being true to yourself in the next action.)

Set out your stall

Whatever you choose to do, make sure you have fun doing it, and do a great job! Make a decision to live by a certain standard, set out your stall, and *never* compromise on it. Stick to your price. As soon as you start to compromise, your standards will slip and your identity will go with it.

You have to decide who you want to be. Do you want to be known as a person who does a rubbish job – or, worse, an average one? You're only ever as good as your last job (or task or project). That's what people will remember you for.

There is nothing more pleasing than seeing your work or help rewarded by somebody really appreciating it, and showing their appreciation by giving you an awesome review or telling their friend how great you are. Nothing spreads more quickly than word of mouth, and generally people only talk about a great experience or a really bad one (check out some book reviews on Amazon to see the truth of this!).

> 'If you having some boundaries and standards is going to "scare" someone away, it's best that they stay scared.'
>
> — Unknown

Having boundaries is just as important as setting out your stall if happiness is your focus. If you don't know how to say no, then it's likely you're a people-pleaser. I used to be one myself. I was a 'yes' man, and what other people thought of me superseded my own happiness. People naturally took advantage of my kind nature (because it happens), and I didn't put enough time or effort into my own happiness.

Now, when I negotiate, I keep going until I hear the word 'no'. I might still push it a little further, but I know when I'm at the limit. Sometimes I don't even want more of a discount – I just negotiate to push the boundaries. If they keep giving me more, I'll most likely take it (like most other people). It's not greed, it's just good negotiation. This is why having boundaries is a must. Most people are just waiting for you to say 'no'. It might be a friend asking you for something they know is testing the boundaries, like being picked up at 2am when they're too drunk to drive. If you're willing to do it, go right ahead. Just be aware that the next call might be at 3am. You have to learn to say no if you want less stress and more happiness.

There's nothing wrong with wanting to be a good friend, but you have to have boundaries. There is a fine line between being nice and being a walkover. Sometimes you have to make a stand. It takes guts, but it's usually rewarded with respect. Your friend will think twice about calling you at 2am (and will instead call somebody else who hasn't established their boundaries), and your boss will ask somebody else to come in to work on their day off.

It's up to you to decide where you want your boundaries to be. Just be mindful: if they are unrealistic, you'll find people won't want to do business with you and you'll have fewer friends. If they are too flexible, people will walk over you. Have a play around to get your balance right. If you feel it is tipping one way or the other, you just need to remind people who you are and where your boundaries lie – by saying no.

Try to make a difference

I used to think I understood what it means to make a difference to people's lives until I started to do it.

Jim Carrey is best known for his wacky acting performances in films including *Ace Ventura*, *The Mask* and *Dumb and Dumber* (my favourite!). As he has such an outrageous persona, you would be forgiven for thinking he's naturally wacky, but there is a surprisingly different side to Jim – a side that I admire immensely.

If you have access to YouTube, watch the video 'The Meaning – Jim Carrey', and you'll see exactly what I mean. In the video Jim speaks about his life, and what he perceives to be the meaning of it. He is deep, caring, spiritual and incredibly warm. I like his views on attracting positive things into your life, and buy into that a lot myself. What I admire most, however, is his genuine love for people. You can see it in his eyes and body language, and hear it in his words – you can't act that. He wants to make a difference in people's lives, and his way is through humour.

Jim summarises the above video by saying that the effect we have on others is the most valuable thing there is. I've come to learn that this is true, and I hope you also get to find out what you can do to make a difference in people's lives. In a professional capacity, I'm blessed to have found this through my books, talks and coaching. In my personal life, I'm able to make Lisa's day better just by making her laugh or supporting her when she needs it. I give my daughter plenty of hugs and kisses and help to shape her life by offering her a little of Daddy's wisdom (even if she can't understand it yet – it keeps me entertained!).

Again, you have a choice. Some people decide to use their gift of influence to cause hurt and pain. There are many reasons for that – but they're not important here. What is important is how you choose to use this gift from this moment forward.

Finding a way to make a difference in people's lives isn't hard. It can start with something as small as a smile. Have you ever had a bad day and then somebody looks at you with a beaming smile, and maybe even says hi to you? It suddenly makes your day feel a whole lot better, doesn't it? You feel that you, too, can make a difference to someone's life with just a smile and a 'hi'.

If you want to go a little deeper (and I suggest you do), there are hundreds of opportunities to volunteer. There are plenty of lonely people out there, and some of them just need some company to make their lives a whole lot better. You could make a difference to somebody's life just by seeing them every now and again to have a chat. If you're an animal lover, you could go to your local sanctuary and walk some dogs, or help look after some cats. You could start a group on social media and get people together. The options are endless.

Helping to make a difference in other people's lives will make all the difference to *your* life. Start small, and the rewards you receive will lead to bigger things. As I said previously, unless you're lucky enough to be financially secure, you will need money to live. I appreciate you can't dedicate all your time for free. I'm not telling you to quit your job here, but suggesting that you start with as little as an hour a week – something everybody can spare. Who knows where it might lead? Who knows who you might meet?

Voluntary work is a great way to meet new people without expectations and the usual 'what can he do for me?' mentality that leads to greed and unhealthy relationships. The key here is meeting people in the right setting, because people make things happen. When you're feeling stuck, meeting new people can get you out of the mire. They can inspire you and lead to action.

If you're feeling stuck right now, it's because you're not meeting enough people (or the right people).

Here are some suggestions for breaking the ice and meeting new people:

- Start smiling and saying hi.
- Start volunteering and meeting new people.
- Start small (just an hour a week), and watch yourself grow.

ACTION 7:
BE TRUE TO YOURSELF AND INVEST IN YOUR #1 ASSET

Chapter 12

Be true to yourself

I'm about to crank up the advice level to the maximum here, so please pay attention to this one! This is one of the pieces of advice that has transformed my life.

If there is one thing I want you to take away from this book, it's: **be true to yourself**. Whenever you don't feel happy, or you are agitated for no apparent reason, or you're just plain miserable, it's often because you're not being true to yourself.

I used to do lots of things because I was following the crowd, rather than following my heart. Holidays, for one. Most of the people I know live for their annual holiday(s). I used to think I was a little strange for not feeling the same. Maybe I am, but most of the holiday experiences I've had have been disappointing. Paying top prices for an average hotel, waiting around in an airport, queuing, being crammed onto a plane, and then suffering jet lag are just a few examples of why I'm not the biggest fan of holidays. My lily-white skin was not made for the sun! I burn very easily and tend to go as red as a lobster. Plus,

I hate sunbathing – I get agitated in the heat. OK, I'm starting to sound miserable, but I'm just being honest!

Of course, there are lots of positives to travelling, but I've come to appreciate I'm just different to most people. It took me a while to appreciate this fact, but I've made peace with it now. Maybe it will change in the future, but right now I'm OK with the fact I'm not rushing to the travel agent to book my next jaunt. I'm being true to myself and feel much better because of it.

Happiness comes from being who you really are

Sometimes we all have to do things we don't want to do, but the trick is to follow your heart and let it guide you. Whether you want to be a CEO or work part-time for a charity, it doesn't matter. What matters is how your goal makes you feel.

The moment you start to deviate or lie is the moment you will fail and be miserable. Other people will only be able to connect with you when you're being yourself – and they will love you for it. If they don't, move on – they weren't right for you anyway.

One of the biggest challenges we face today is being who we really want to be. We're influenced by endless external sources (such as the media and popular TV programmes) to wear the right clothes, drive the right car, look a certain way, and be the next A-list celeb. Money drives all these things, and the perception is that the more money you have, the better life will be. I learned the hard way that this is absolute rubbish.

I'm not saying there's anything wrong with wanting to have a better life (whether this means having more material possessions, high career aspirations or improving your appearance). What I am saying is that there is a thin line between being grateful for what you've got and suffering from stress because a celebrity has told you you're not quite thin enough. Only you know when you're crossing that thin line. Anxiety and stress are normally a sign that you are.

It's OK to feel anxious about not fitting in, but if it's causing you stress, you need to look at why. Are you doing what you do just to try and keep up with everybody else? Are you worrying about your weight because a celebrity you admire is thinner than you are? Is that making you happy? Probably not, if you're reading this book.

Play to your strengths

Being true to yourself also means playing to your strengths. You are who you are, and you're not going to change. You can educate yourself and continue to strive to be a better version of you, but your core will always remain, including the things you're not so good at. That's why you have to identify – and play to – your strengths as much as you possibly can.

If you're naturally good at something, keep doing it. That will be your ticket to a less-stress lifestyle. You're better off using this strategy than spending time improving your weaknesses. Trying to get better at things you're really not good at takes way too much time and effort, compared to being super-good at the things you're already good at. The reason top entrepreneurs say 'have a great team around you' and 'employ better people than yourself' is because they appreciate they can't be great at everything, and they employ others to fill the skills gap.

I'm good at selling, but awful at things that require analysis, such as online marketing. I haven't got the patience for it. Since I'm a control freak, I want to be good at everything, so I spent ages trying to work out search engine optimisation (SEO), how best to use Google, and all the other online stuff they say you need to master. I spent weeks wading through tips and advice on what this website should say, why I should backlink to this site, and where I should share information. With hindsight, my time would have been much better spent playing to my strengths, like selling the product. I'm never going to be an SEO expert (and don't want to be!), so I wasn't spending my time productively. If I had concentrated on selling (something I enjoy), I would have continued to get better at selling, which can only be a good thing. I enjoy it more, get a greater sense of fulfilment from it, and therefore feel much happier doing it.

If you're really not good at something, don't waste your time on it. Fill the gap with somebody that is good at it. If you hate doing a particular task, think: do you know somebody who would love to do it?

Don't compare yourself to others

One of the biggest mistakes I've made in the past is comparing myself to others. It's something none of us can avoid because we all seek approval. It's something I work on daily, but because I'm now aware of it, I'm a lot better than I used to be.

You only have to think back to your school days to understand this point. There are always the 'cool' kids and the 'outsiders'. We're categorised as one or the other, and there isn't much in between. This labelling continues into our adult years. To try and fit in, we overcompensate by showing others how great we are, often by buying houses, cars, and other material possessions. There is nothing wrong with wanting to have nice things in life, but if you're buying these things to impress others (and you usually are), you'll struggle to draw happiness from that.

A lot of social media is used for this exact reason. I don't have a personal Facebook account, but I know a lot of people who do. The main aim of many people is to show others how great their lives are. They can't just go and have a nice day out – they have to show everybody else how great their day out is. Again, there's nothing wrong with wanting to share happiness, but when posting about their day is more important than enjoying the day, then they have a problem.

Another big concern of mine is the 'we should look a certain way otherwise we're not acceptable' mentality, which is usually driven by celebrities. And it's not just teens who are being sucked in. In fact, it seems that, the older we get, the more pressure we're under to look younger (both men and women). If an A-list celebrity comes out and says that huge bums are 'in', all of a sudden bum implants are the next big thing. I fail to see where the joy in this is. Equally, if you're overweight, then that's a health issue that you should address. You shouldn't lose weight if a celebrity tells you to – you should do it because your doctor tells you to!

Do yourself a favour and stop comparing yourself to others: stop following celebrities, stop feeling as though you have to show everybody how great your life is, and get on with living it. Whether you're on social media or not, your true friends will always be there, and will love you for who you are. A thousand friends on Facebook means very little when you don't connect with real-life friends.

You don't have to justify anything you do to anybody (except the police and your mum, of course). You are you, you are individual, and you are special. You were made that way, so start embracing it.

Be your own mentor

When I started out on my quest for self-improvement, one of the best pieces of advice I was consistently given was to find a mentor. Although I think it's imperative to learn from others, whether from a mentor, friend, family member or business associate, I believe it's more important to learn from yourself.

Have you noticed how many different ways there are to achieve the same thing? Which one of those ways is right if they all achieve the same? The thing that is quickest and cheapest? Maybe. But what if you follow that, and it makes you miserable? Is it worth it? It might be for somebody else, but what about you?

My point is that there will always be different ways to accomplish the same thing. Virgin will offer one thing, British Airways another, but they'll both fly to the same destination. Conflicting advice on how to achieve something will frazzle your brain! An expert will recommend you do *x*, and another expert will say you should do *y* instead. For example, have you seen how many different books there are on dieting?

What do you do? Whose advice do you take? Which way do you turn?

You go in the direction that is most true to yourself, and therefore the one that makes you most happy, no matter how much advice you're given.

I look up to certain people for different reasons. Some have influenced me more than others, and because of this, I've found myself sometimes trying to mimic what they do. If they're successful, there's nothing wrong with me doing this, right? Not entirely. We naturally want to emulate the people we most admire, but this can sometimes be to our detriment. If you try to be somebody you're not, you'll be found out in the end – either because you'll be unhappy or because you'll fail.

If there is an area in your life that you know needs work, work on it bearing in mind who you are. If you try to work on it by mimicking somebody else, you won't succeed. If you want happiness and true success, stick to being you.

If you look up to Steve Jobs, it doesn't mean you have to speak to people with contempt to get things done. If you look up to Richard Branson, it doesn't mean you have to run hundreds of companies in different sectors to be wealthy. If you look up to Gordon Ramsay, it doesn't mean you have to swear like a trooper. Success will come from who you are – not from somebody else.

It's always better to be the real thing than a tribute act. Be your own mentor, and be yourself.

Stick to your values

Whenever you're not sure what to do next, go back to your values. This won't only get you out of feeling stuck; it will enable you to be yourself, and therefore be truly happy. Your values are your core beliefs (your standards and morals), and the values I mean here are the things we all believe in – such as honesty, fairness, compassion, truthfulness. The standards that are most important to you will be unique to you. Adhering to your values does you good and benefits the people around you.

If your morals are unscrupulous, such as being dishonest and deceitful, the end product will be counterfeiting and fraud. If this is the case, I wish you well in prison. You can either strive to be the next Adidas, or you can spend your time trying to counterfeit their goods. It's your choice.

Remember, there are hundreds of different ways to accomplish the same thing. How do you find the way that is right for you? By sticking to your values. Your values will change as you experience new things and progress through life, but the backbone of who you are will always remain. You don't go from supporting one football team to another (unless you're a glory supporter!), so don't do the same thing with what makes you, you. Stick to your values if you want success and happiness.

Go back to your values to identify what you need to do. It may well be different from the crowd, and you might be sticking up for the odd one out, but if it feels right, it is. In other words, your values might be different to everybody else's – but if you want a different result to everybody else, this is a good thing. For example, I will never offer a money-back guarantee on anything I do. Why? Because it goes against my values. If you buy something from me, it's because I want you to buy it, not because you buy it and regret it later on. Most of my competitors will offer a money-back guarantee because they know it will sell more of what they are selling, and it's a tried-and-tested marketing technique. I don't care if I don't sell as much – I'm being true to myself, I'm sticking to my values, and I'm happy because of it.

If you do something, and it doesn't feel right, it's because you're not being true to yourself: you're going against your values.

Businesses and lives are built on values. They help to elevate individuals to new levels. They set precedents and spark change. They beat competing firms that don't have any values. A company that has a culture built on values, like a mission statement that they do business by, is much more likely to succeed than a business without one. Virgin Atlantic's mission statement is 'to embrace the human spirit and let it fly'. It's my favourite airline to fly with, and Richard Branson is doing OK for himself, right?

If you don't have values, it's about time you got some.

Chapter 13

Invest in your #1 asset

There is an investment you can make that consistently outstrips the stock market and makes the housing market look insignificant. If you back it, it will never let you down. You only need to give it a little encouragement and belief, and it will flourish and accomplish unimaginable things. Get your pen and paper ready for the biggest tip you'll get this century:

The best investment you will ever make is in yourself.

Invest in yourself – because if you don't, nobody else will. Somebody will always be waiting to shape your life for you (a boss, business owner, shareholder or spouse). Investing in yourself is the only sure-fire way to achieve what you want out of life.

Be a leader

The reason most of us follow the crowd is that it's easier. It's easier to be told what to do rather than work it out for ourselves. We don't want a boss, but we're often too lazy to make decisions and take responsibility for our own lives (because, again, this takes effort). The truth is, many of us wouldn't know what to do if we didn't have a boss.

Creating a less-stress lifestyle requires you to be a leader, and break through this laziness. You have to step forward and be prepared to take responsibility, even if it means things might go wrong. You can't have your cake and eat it! Expecting somebody else to map out your future, and relying on a company or a partner for security leaves the door wide open to disappointment and failure.

If you don't take charge of life now, when you get older there's a risk that you'll play the blame game, blaming your ex-partner, the government, your company, your career, or even your family and friends for the fact things didn't turn out right for you. There is only one person you can rely on to secure your future and make sure this doesn't happen, and that's you. That's why it's worth making the effort to take responsibility and become the leader in your life.

You don't have to do anything drastic to start being a leader. It can start with something as simple as making more decisions. The next time you go out with friends to a restaurant and the waitress asks you, 'Would you like to order wine?', rather than the usual umming and ahhing and debate, immediately take charge: 'Yes, I'd like wine. Who else would like wine?' Take the menu and take control. It develops your leadership skills, builds your confidence and helps you practise being a leader. The more you practise being a leader, the better you'll get at it. You'll stop depending on others to make decisions for you.

Leaders are leaders because they take charge. They lead from the front. All top performers are leaders. Not all of them are natural leaders, but through practice, they've developed the skills required to be the best.

As I said earlier, you are whatever you believe you can be. When you believe you can be a leader, and start acting like a leader, you'll become one.

Don't stop learning

Read, attend courses, watch your business and lifestyle idols. Gordon Ramsay is one of my idols because I'm a fan of both cooking and entrepreneurship (which is just as well because I do swear nearly as much as he does – I've tried not to in this book!). When I watch his TV programmes, they inspire me to learn.

If you're in the car, make it your university by listening to audio books. What worked for me was cancelling satellite TV. There were so many channels that I found myself spending hours flicking through them, not watching anything in particular. What a waste of precious time!

I can now get through half a book in that time, and guess which activity gives me a brighter future and the tools to be happier and less stressed?

If you're not using your brain, it will retire. It will go into a deep sleep. It's an organ that acts like a muscle and, like all your other muscles, if you don't use it, it will wither away. Give it the constant challenge and variety it deserves. I always have a game or two of chess on the go on my phone. It keeps my brain ticking over, so I feel focused and sharp. There are lots of other activities that can keep you sharp, too. If you have a smartphone, check out all the apps in the game section – this is a great solution because you can carry your games around with you at all times. If you're on the train, waiting in a queue or just bored sitting at home, get your games out and start playing. (Just don't get addicted – that's counterproductive to your less-stress lifestyle!)

If you're not learning, you're not growing, and if you're not growing, you're dying. This is the cycle of life. Everybody has the opportunity to expand their capabilities – and it's through learning you'll do this.

Your main weapon in the fight to be top is intelligence. Grab a book, listen to an audio book, go on a course – these things are your arsenal.

Be super niche

Whatever you choose to do, whether it's starting your own venture or doing some blogging for fun, start by being super niche. In other words, find a subject, and then find something within that subject you can focus on.

The world is overloaded with information, and a lot of it is rubbish. Take Google, for example. Google has a team and system dedicated to sorting the useful from the rubbish, but the rubbish is still there, and it will keep coming. You have to view your strategy very much in the same way. How are you going to differentiate yourself from the rubbish? Apart from the obvious, like having something somebody wants, the only way you can do it in today's competitive market is by being super niche.

There is no point in inventing the next great sports drink and trying to pitch it to the entire sports drink audience with a £10,000 start-up budget. If you haven't got millions to invest (and you can't afford to risk losing money), then you need to be super focused on your audience. In this instance (a sports drink), you might target people who play an unusual sport: 'This drink helps you play [niche sport] because . . .'. Your £10,000 start-up budget will stretch further, and is much more likely to work using this strategy.

You don't have to stay niche. This strategy is about proving something works, getting stories from others about how it's helped them, and building a reputation. You can use the profit to move into other areas. It is a slower-moving strategy than ploughing millions into something, but most of us haven't got millions to do that. You have to start somewhere, right? Otherwise, if you get too caught up in 'thinking big', you might never start anything new.

Ask for feedback

When we think of feedback we typically think of a company survey, but asking for feedback in all parts of your life will help you grow in every aspect – so don't be afraid to ask for feedback.

Ask your partner what you can do to be a better lover. Ask your children what you can do to be a better parent. (If they are two years old they will look at you blankly then throw something at you, so it's probably best to wait until they're in their teens!) Ask your friends what you can do to be a better friend. Ask your customers what you can do to provide a better service. You get the idea. You'll find that people will be queuing up to give you feedback – they love it. Listen to the feedback and utilise it – it's your key to a better way of living.

Big businesses know how powerful feedback is. Have you noticed, whenever you buy something from Amazon or another big company, you're asked for feedback? Or when you've spoken to somebody at Apple they'll send you an email to ask about their customer service? Businesses like these know that they can use our feedback to make their business better. We're telling them exactly what they need to be doing.

When Gordon Ramsay was building his restaurant empire, he always listened to negative comments from his customers, rather than grow his ego with the good ones. He knew that listening to the negative stuff and acting on it would improve his restaurants and he would gain an edge over his competition.

If you want to be great, and not just good, listen to the bad stuff. You won't please everybody (and you don't want to), but the negatives hold the key to greatness. Like Gordon, use people's anger and frustration to make the changes that will take you to new levels. Ignore feedback from people who're just having a bad day. You'll spot the difference.

Feedback is a powerful tool and, like I say, you shouldn't limit it to just business. If you're not currently asking for feedback, start today, and aim to get feedback in every aspect of your life – it will give you an advantage without having to spend time or money. The people providing the feedback are doing all the hard work; all you need to do is listen.

How much are you willing to invest?

This is a serious question: how much are you willing to invest? The reason I ask is that the more you invest in yourself, the more you'll get out of life – it really is that simple.

If you watch TV all day, instead of learning a new skill that can take your life to the next level, you won't go to the next level. I know you already know this, but, if that's the case, why do most of us sit watching brain-dead TV rather than do the things we know can improve our lives? Laziness? Maybe. Taking the easy option? Maybe. There are a ton of reasons, but I believe the underlying reason is fear: the fear of change – the fear that things could change for the better if you start investing in your future. Sometimes change is exactly what we need, and embracing it is the best thing we can do.

It may well be that after eight hours in the office the last thing you want to do is come home and read or learn a new skill. I completely get it, and I've been there. But, here's where I take out my 'kick up the butt' shoes. If you keep following that same pattern of coming home from work and sitting in front of the TV, your life won't change – it will stay the same. Excuses like 'I'm not a reader' or 'I've got a short attention span' don't wash either.

If you don't invest in your future, it will look the same in three years' time. Change won't happen, and you'll be stuck doing the same things you've always done. To change, you need to be prepared to invest in yourself.

If you were to give your life an overall rating out of ten right now, what would it be? Five, six, maybe seven? Let's say it's seven. What are you going to do to get it to ten? Why not make a list of things that you could do to improve your life?

If you want top results, you have to put in the effort. That means pushing yourself and making sacrifices. Turn the TV off and pick up the book. Put the second piece of cake down – you don't need it. Start a passive income strategy plan (we'll come on to this in Chapter 17). Sacrifice isn't forever, and is normally front-loaded – there are usually lots of rewards waiting for you in return; you just have to be a little patient.

Invest in yourself to get the most out of life and feel great.

I'll say it again: the effort you put into learning, and your commitment, will match your results. The more you put in, the more you'll get out of life.

ACTION 8:
FIND ENDLESS PASSION

Chapter 14

Find endless passion

When every successful and happy person I read about consistently said 'find your passion' and 'do what you love', I thought I understood it. They are clear enough statements, but it turns out I didn't understand them at all. I got so tired of having these types of statements shoved down my throat that I became bitter towards them, especially if I was having a bad day. I used to read them and think, 'It's OK for you to say that, you've got a ton of money so you get to follow your passion and do what you love.' It used to annoy me rather than inspire me. Now, I completely get it – I was looking at it all wrong.

At times, life is going to kick you in the ass. People are going to let you down and things will go wrong unexpectedly. One of the few things that will get you through this inevitability is **passion** – doing what you love. It's one of the big differences between success and failure. If you haven't got a passion for what you do, somebody else will always do it better than you. Even if you don't think your lack of passion is visible, people have a way of smelling it!

You see it every day – very average things that do very well, and great things that fail. If you watch *Dragons' Den,* you'll have seen it for yourself. Cooking sauces, clothing ranges, and inventions that aren't much better than what is already on the market but which make a fortune. There are lots of factors that dictate that, such as TV exposure and the right backing, but passion will always be at the heart of it. That's why you don't necessarily need a good idea for it to work, or Prince Charming looks to bag your princess – average becomes great when you throw in bags of passion.

I've discovered few things that offer endless passion, but there is one thing that, if you crack it, will offer you as much passion as you seek.

If you want endless passion, look at changing people's lives.

Ask yourself, what can I do to improve other people's lives? What do I know that can help other people? What skills do I possess that can make a real difference to people's lives? These are not easy questions to answer, so take your time, but getting the answers right will be worth it when you get genuine feedback from people you have inspired – people like you and me who need to hear the right thing at the right time.

I can't think of anything else better than helping other people. There is no greater reward or career than passing on knowledge. If you're lucky enough to find the answers to the above, you'll discover why too.

As I've mentioned, making a start is one of the hardest things to do. So, here's something to get the ball rolling. Think about your life, including all the tough times you've been through. How did you get from point A to point B? In other words, how did you overcome that rough patch? What did you do? What did you have to change? Did you have a process? You now have something to share with others going through the same thing – because you can guarantee there will always be somebody else experiencing what you've been through who needs your help.

Find your cause

I don't believe everybody has a calling. I believe that we're all put in different situations, and the people with passion and enough will to make a difference will succeed. Whether that situation is being born into poverty or with more wealth than they know what to do with, the people with passion will be the ones who do special things.

Money alone will never be enough. If you're always chasing a bigger house, a better car or a fancier boat, you will never be happy or free. You have to have something else to work towards – a cause – otherwise things will get mundane and pointless.

A life without substance is no life at all. Avoiding the quick fix of happiness is a great start to finding substance. I've seen it a million times – people jumping from job to job because they believe the grass is greener elsewhere. Somebody having an affair because their relationship has become stale. Whatever the quick fix, the honeymoon period never lasts.

Only you know what your cause is – nobody can tell you what it is. It's up to you to discover it (if you haven't already). It's not easy, though. If it were that easy, we'd all be living fabulous lives. To help you find yours, here are a few quick starter questions:

- What makes you passionate? What puts a fire in your belly?
- What excites you?
- When were you last happiest? What were you doing?

If you're fed up, these questions might wind you up rather than help you find your cause (I know, I've been there!). But, if you were to answer one, I'd start with the first – what makes you passionate? Passion is the route to finding your cause.

Here's the irony: you could probably spend a lifetime looking for your cause and not find it. The good news is your cause normally has a way of finding you. That doesn't mean if you sit at home all day it will come knocking on your door. Let me rephrase: Don't waste your time chasing your cause; keep following your passion and it will find you.

Mix it up

A good friend of mine is a dentist. He spent many years training to become a dentist. His father was a dentist, and he wanted his son to follow in his footsteps. Having high expectations for his son, he paid for his education and helped set him up with his own practice. Thanks, Dad!

My friend has now been a dentist for over ten years, running his own successful practice and winning acclamations for his work in dentistry. Luckily, he has a natural talent and passion for dentistry, but here's the thing (you knew something was coming!): like anybody else, he gets bored! It's hard to stay passionate when you're doing the same things over and over again. It's extra difficult when you've trained in something for many years (such as dentistry, medicine or law), and even more difficult when your parent has paid for it and has high expectations for you.

The fact is, whether we're trained in a profession or not, we all get bored. So, how do you break through and overcome this boredom? You mix it up!

What do I mean by mixing it up? Keep doing what you're doing, but put things in place that can help you create your less-stress lifestyle – things you've learned from this book. This should give you enough of a challenge to get your passion back and prevent further boredom.

We aren't robots. We're sentient beings. We get bored! Passion isn't easy to sustain. You're not weak, and you're certainly not a failure for recognising you need something new. Trying to ignore your feelings will only lead to misery, so you're doing the right thing by looking for new challenges.

It's almost always a bad idea to make a rash decision. Sometimes mixing it up is all you need to do. Things can change as you move forward, and as your circumstances alter you can look to make big decisions when the time is right – when you don't feel forced or desperate. Pressure and desperation usually lead to bad decision-making.

Spinning more plates does require harder work, to begin with, but the initial extra stress is worth it in the long run – as long as you're keeping tabs on it. It's important to get the balance right between what you're currently doing and achieving your longer-term goals because having too many things on the go at once can make you feel out of control. If you end up having a mental breakdown, you've defeated the object.

Plan and grow organically

For me, the opposite of passion is disheartenment. The quickest way to get disheartened is to keep starting over and over again from scratch. If you keep trying new ideas and never see any through, you'll keep going back to square one, and that's not good. It's the quickest route to dejection and failure.

In my early years, I had lots of business ideas, most of which were never going to succeed. With a lack of experience and guidance (but endless vigour), I'd jump into things without planning them correctly, and would end up failing pretty quickly. Out of ten things I tried, one maybe had some legs. This is a pretty typical story for a budding entrepreneur, but it deserves attention. Why? Because, like so many other people, I nearly gave up on my dream of freedom. I got so fed up with failing that I nearly resigned myself to a life surviving from pay cheque to pay cheque.

The moral of the story isn't to stop trying new things; it's to plan correctly and stick to something. You have to let your idea grow roots; otherwise, it will be pulled out of the ground and tossed aside too easily. I have no doubt more of my ideas would have come off earlier if I'd put more planning into them and stuck at them longer, and had a better strategy.

The best strategy is to chip away at the mountain, rather than to try moving it in its entirety. This is where organic growth comes in. If I'd started blogging when I was twenty, and written a new blog every other day, I'd have much higher rankings on Google (and potentially a lot more followers) than I have today.

> 'Take care of the minutes, and the hours will take care of themselves.'
>
> — Lord Chesterfield, 'Letters to his Son' (1739)

I've noticed that the 'want it yesterday' mentality common in the younger generation is causing a lot of people to fail. Slow, sure and organic will always beat a rush job (think of the story of the hare and the tortoise).

It's never too late to start. You just have to take the first step. Things will never grow organically if they are not planted in the first place. What you're doing today is making the difference for tomorrow. If you're not sure what your future looks like, what is your life like, right now? What are you eating today? How much exercise are you getting? How many hours are you investing in yourself? The answers to these questions will give you all the information you need.

Offer free advice

In future, don't go into anything with money as the focus. Money is a by-product of passion, and passion should take the lead. If you focus on only the money, it won't work. If it does, it rarely leads to endless passion and happiness.

I offer lots of free advice on my blog (at www.carlvernon.com), and I'm more than happy to share all my ideas, even the best ones. I don't see the point in holding back for fear of people copying me. You will always get copied. I've had people copy me all my life. It used to annoy me, but now I see it as a positive – imitation is the highest compliment I could be paid. (If it's blatant copying with no regard for copyright laws, however, that's what we have courts for!)

If you think about it, everything exists already anyway (very philosophical, Carl!), so we have no choice but to replicate existing ideas. Everything is borrowed, otherwise, how would we learn?

However, I do believe in originality. You can only go out and try and replicate to a point before you're either found out or the pioneer wipes you out of the market. Like when Virgin Cola tried to compete with Coca-Cola in 1994. Richard Branson wanted his brand to be as big as Coca-Cola, and he spent an eye-watering amount to make it happen. Richard Branson's achievements are undeniable, but even he bit off more than he could chew when he tried to compete in this space. Coca-Cola, being the pioneer, wiped the floor with him.

The crucial factor here is **execution**. I know I can put free information out into the public domain, and if I felt passionate enough about something to make it happen, I'd execute it better than somebody else. That's the thing about originality – you can't replicate and successfully execute someone else's story; it has to be yours.

Find your own story, and share it. There won't be anybody else who will execute it as well as you, even if you share your best ideas for free.

ACTION 9:
ORGANISE YOUR LIFE AND MANAGE YOUR ENVIRONMENT

Chapter 15

Streamline, automate and organise (SAO!)

We've all heard about SEO (search engine optimisation), but if you want a less-stress lifestyle, you've got to start looking at SAO: Streamline, Automate and Organise!

So much of our stress is caused by being disorganised, feeling out of control, and feeling as if we have too much to do and not enough time to do it. The solution is SAO, so let's have a look at some of the things you can do to achieve this.

The Pareto principle

The Pareto principle (also known as the 80/20 rule) says that 80% of effects come from 20% of causes. In other words, two out of the ten things you're doing right now in your life are working for you and contributing to all of your success, and eight out of ten things you're doing are potentially wasting your time and effort.

I decided to put this principle to the test, using my recruitment company as the guinea pig. Over three months, I analysed what I was doing and what was taking up my time. The results were very interesting! It proved to me that the Pareto principle is pretty damn accurate.

When I wrote down all my clients' names, including the fees I'd earned from them, I noticed there were only a few who actually made my business profitable. Out of my top ten clients, only two were worth my effort. The rest of my clients were sucking the life out of me and putting a dent in my profit. Based on these findings, I decided to drop these clients and concentrate on the two who made me money. This was one of the best business decisions I'd ever made. Overnight, my workload dropped by three-quarters, and all of a sudden I had more time to concentrate on other, more meaningful things – like writing this book! – while sustaining the same profit levels.

On reflection, I was just filling my time for the sake of doing it. It was almost as though I was using the other timewasting and non-profitable clients as an excuse to fill my working day. The usual thinking is that, unless you're working at least eight hours a day, you're not productive. In some circumstances, this might be accurate, but in a lot it's not. *What* you're doing is more important than how long you're doing it for.

This principle worked so well that I decided to adopt it in other aspects of my life. I analysed what my typical week looked like and, once again, noticed that about 80% of my personal time was being wasted, mostly with TV. It was only about 20% of what I was doing that was contributing to my personal growth: mostly reading (learning), writing, exercising and cooking (my passion). Again, having analysed the results, I decided to up my 20% productive time and decrease the 80% waste of time. I started to learn more by increasing my reading time and listening to more audio books, wrote more of my book, exercised more often, and ate more healthily because I cooked more fresh food – I even started to find more time to socialise and do more of the things that kept me happy, like spending quality time with my family. Thank you, Pareto principle!

You can do the same exercise. What does your week look like? What is the 80% you're wasting your time on? How can you limit these activities? What is the 20% that is making a difference in your life, and allowing you to grow? Can you increase these activities – and find more?

I've made a note on my calendar on the last day of each month that says 'Pareto'. It reminds me to analyse my lifestyle continually and use the principle to maximise my time. It might also help you do the same. Give it a try!

Say no

When I worked in sales, the biggest problem I faced was gatekeepers. If you're in sales, you'll know what I mean. If you're not, gatekeepers are the people who stop you from talking to the decision-makers. They're usually receptionists or PAs. Gatekeepers took up 80% of my time and, although they were annoying, I understand why they're there. The decision-maker has a job to do, and can't just take sales calls all day. If they did that, they would never get their job done, and they would probably be seriously depressed from having to listen to endless cold callers!

You are your own decision-maker, and because most of us aren't lucky enough to have our own gatekeeper, you have to be strict with your time. More importantly, you have to possess the ability to say no.

Life, if you let it, will drag you from pillar to post. This is just another way of saying 'if you let people take advantage of you, you'll be torn apart'. If somebody says they really need you urgently (apart from a life-or-death situation), it's normally to suit their own needs. Do they *really* need you? Or are they just trying to make their own lives easier? Remember, give somebody an inch and they'll take a mile.

It's time to start dictating your own agenda, and stop following everybody else's. If you haven't got your own agenda and a plan, that's exactly what you'll be doing, and you can guarantee people will be taking advantage of you. It's not easy to do, especially if you have a kind nature, but you have to practise saying no more often. Saying no will free up more of your time than you ever thought possible.

If tomorrow you said yes to everything that was asked of you, imagine what your day would look like. You wouldn't have time for lunch because of the extra calls you would have to make, you would finish work way after you're supposed to, and when you got home, it wouldn't end because you would have to carry out all the demands your children made of you (rather than most of them!). It would be a nightmare of endless tasks!

The reason most of us end up living average lives is because we get bogged down by the average tasks we're asked to do. Performing average tasks becomes our life, and our lives become average because of it. If you focus your time on low-value tasks, you'll get a low-value life in return. If you want a less-stress lifestyle, you have to prioritise tasks that will make a difference to your life – and that requires the ability to say no.

For a long time I felt that I couldn't afford a cleaner or gardener. Plus, for a working-class lad like me, it wasn't the norm. That was, until I decided to give it a go. Both the physical time and mental space (emotional attachment) I freed up by delegating these tasks was worth a lot more than the fair price I was paying my cleaner and gardener.

By delegating these tasks, I could prioritise and focus on the highest-value tasks in my life and work on them, knowing that everything else was getting done. When the car needs a clean, rather than spend my Sunday morning doing it, I'll get it valeted while I'm writing or doing something I know is taking my life forward. If you feel these examples are extreme, and there is nothing wrong with doing a bit of gardening or cleaning, you're right – but let me ask you a question: are you achieving what you want to achieve in your life?

Every second counts – as long as you're making them count. You can choose to keep doing average tasks, and therefore have an average life, or you can use your time to learn something new that will elevate your life. If you think the cost of a cleaner or gardener isn't worth it, look again.

The 80/20 rule has helped me to be more productive with my time by focusing on the tasks that count, and saying no has helped me pinpoint this focus even further. Use them together, and they will build a barrier that nobody can get past!

Automate your learning

If you're not growing and evolving as a person, you're withering away. Learning allows continual growth, and if you're constantly learning you're growing. Let's have a look at some ways you can automate your learning and make it as easy and painless as possible.

Subscribe to blogs and mailing lists

Subscribe to blogs and mailing lists on subjects that interest you. Get information coming to you, rather than spending tons of time going out and looking for it. Limit your subscriptions to a few, enough to keep your reading light so you don't feel overwhelmed. Make sure it's quality content, so you're not wasting your time.

I subscribe to four or five blogs and mailing lists, with my top two being Seth Godin's blog (http://sethgodin.typepad.com/) and Entrepreneur (https://www.entrepreneur.com). Seth is a best-selling author and marketing genius. His blog is one of the most popular blogs in the world – and it's unique. He sends out a blog every day, but it's just a short one, sometimes only a few sentences. For me, it serves as a daily inspiration. He's one of the reasons I started writing. I also get an email every week or so from Entrepreneur which is just as inspirational. It lists the top posts of that week, which are quick to read and full of useful information for any aspiring or accomplished entrepreneur. The others I get are based on my hobbies, like poker and property.

There's no point learning how to make money if you don't know what to spend it on, right?

Audio books

I rarely read a book, mainly because I'm such a slow reader. It takes me weeks to get through one book. I did some research into speed-reading, but couldn't get on with it – I can't take in the information. Audio books offer the perfect solution. I can get through a book in hours and combine it with other things, like exercise and driving. The last time I checked, it wasn't safe – or legal – to drive while reading, and sometimes I can be on the road for hours at a time. I can either use this time to listen to pop on the radio – or learn. I choose the latter and make my car a university. Same with the gym: I pop my headphones in and before I know it I've completed half a book in one session – and become healthier at the same time. Can't be bad!

Here's a tip for listening to audio books: depending on the speed of the narrator's voice, I put the speed up to twice the normal speed of the audio book. It takes a bit of getting used to, but it's not long before normal audio speed sounds like it's on slow-mo. At twice the speed, a six-hour audio turns into a three-hour one, leaving plenty more time for learning and doing other productive things!

Ask somebody else

We're going to cover influence more in a second, but getting somebody else to do the legwork for you can speed up and automate your learning tenfold.

I rarely watch the news, and I don't remember the last time I bought a newspaper. This is out of choice, because I find the news so damn depressing! I'll ask the people around me if there is anything significant I need to know, and anything significant enough usually comes up in conversation anyway. I save hours not rooting through a newspaper, and choose what I want to learn, rather than it being chosen for me.

I'm much happier not watching the news every day. Try it for yourself. Naivety really is bliss.

Influence

Dale Carnegie's book *How to Win Friends and Influence People* is a best-seller. Why? Because knowing how to influence people can make our lives a whole lot easier.

If you were to highlight some of the key qualities of highly successful, happy people, influence is way up there. Imagine the power of being able to get people to do things for you, especially things you don't want to do. Well, I'm pleased to tell you, it's not as hard as you might think. I'm not talking about taking advantage or manipulation – I'm talking about simple psychology. Sometimes it's as simple as asking.

Let's use selling as an example, seeing as sales and influence are very much entwined. The thing that separates a top salesperson from an average one is their ability to ask for something, and not being afraid to ask for it. Nobody likes to be rejected, and it's this fear that prevents us from asking for what we want: from asking somebody for their phone number, or for a pay rise, for example.

This is why alcohol is so popular – it lowers our inhibitions and gives us the Dutch courage to do things we wouldn't normally do. Top salespeople don't need alcohol because they harness the skill of influence. They take – and look at – rejection differently from most people, and it doesn't bother them as much. *So she said no. Who cares? I'll move on to the next.*

The reason you need to get better at influencing is because it can seriously streamline, automate and organise your life. How? By something I've already mentioned – getting people to do things for you.

Masters of influence literally have people queuing up to do things for them. How? Because people *want* to do things for them. The master influencer uses our need for approval and our inbuilt instinct to help others with absolute precision.

If you want to harness the skill of influence more for yourself (and you should), a good start might be Dale Carnegie's book, although there are plenty of similar books out there. If you want to jump straight into it, I have a basic technique for you to try. The next time you need something doing, ask the person you have chosen by using their name: 'Fred, I was hoping you could help me . . .' or 'Alison, I really need your help . . .'. (If you know someone's name, always use it for a more personal touch.) It's in our instinct to want to help others, and if you ask directly for help, it's hard for the other person not to comply.

I'm not into trickery or mind games, but techniques like this are just basic psychology. If they can help get you where you need to be, and they don't hurt anybody in the process, they should be part of your armoury on the path to your less-stress lifestyle.

Measure your actions, goals and results

If you were asked to put up a set of curtains, you wouldn't go out and buy a set without measuring the window first. Why? Because you'll want to make sure they cover the window, and that they don't look ridiculous by overflowing onto the floor. This is a simple example, but it highlights why we should plan in everyday life.

When I was employing people, one of the biggest mistakes I made was giving them too much freedom. I know this sounds contradictory to what my aim is for you (freedom), but I have the benefit of seeing it from both sides (as an employer and employee). I know, as an employer, it's impossible to give your staff complete freedom because of the point I'm about to cover. This proves the point that, if you want absolute freedom, it can only be achieved on your own terms.

I used to embrace people as individuals, and gave them as much freedom as I could, to allow their qualities to shine through. There's nothing wrong with this, but then it started to backfire on me.

My competitors were quickly burning their staff out, so I thought that if I was more flexible with targets it would limit my staff's stress by allowing them to embrace freedom. Two of the ten staff did exactly that and exceeded any targets that would have been given to them. The other eight didn't know what to do with their freedom and completely lost their way. On reflection, I can understand why. If you're not blessed with an abundance of self-drive and ability (and a lot of people aren't, hence the eight out of ten stat), how are you going to know what you're doing is right or expected if you don't measure it?

We need guidance to perform well, both in business and life. We need to know what's expected of us, and we can only do that by measuring – measuring our actions, goals and results.

I'll put my hand up and admit this is a real weakness of mine. I'm not an analyst, and the idea of sitting down to study a spreadsheet bores me. This is why I try and automate the process as much as I can. I use software and set up spreadsheets that make calculations for me. If I use a service, like advertising, I get them to feed back results to me and, based on the results, I decide if I want to continue using them.

Utilise and embrace software as much as you can, and save time wherever possible. Make sure you measure everything you do. It's the only way you're going to know if you need to make a change, ditch something, or increase your investment in it. It's the only way you're going to know if you're achieving what you expect to achieve.

Protect, back up, and live in the cloud

In case you're not familiar with the term 'in the cloud' or 'cloud storage', it means a method of keeping data and files safe and accessible without the need for a physical storage drive. For example, if you needed to run software between computers in a business, the 'old' way of doing it required a physical server present in the office. The problem with this 'old' way is obvious – if anything happened to the server, it usually shut your business down while you repaired it (this has happened to me). With the 'new' cloud-based systems, you don't need any physical data storage because your software is 'in the cloud'. ('The cloud' in this instance is usually a secure building somewhere in the world designed to house high-tech servers that serve many businesses.) Anyway, enough of the boring, technical stuff. All you need to know is that you need to be in the cloud!

The cloud offers you the flexibility to work anywhere at any time, and as long as you have an internet connection, you're in business. When you lose your phone or laptop, you won't lose your photos and documents that are important to you, because you will have uploaded them safely to the cloud. And that's what I like best about the cloud – its flexibility and security. It allows you to be flexible and doesn't tie you down to expensive computers, servers, software and subscriptions. All these things help to free space in your mind by limiting your emotional attachments, and therefore reducing your stress.

You don't need to be a large corporate business to make the cloud work for you. There are small everyday applications you can use that can help with SAO. Below I list a few examples, but I suggest you embrace anything that will streamline, automate and organise your life, including all forms of technology that will make your life easier. If you have to pay, and you think it's too expensive, look deeper. How much time will it save you? Remember, your time is everything. Repetitive tasks present opportunities to create a less-stress lifestyle because there is normally some form of technology that provides a solution for it. Look for processes that can help you achieve this. For its flexibility and security benefits, I recommend the cloud.

Outlook/Google Calendar

I use Outlook as a calendar to help me organise my time and get tasks done. If you don't have access to Outlook, there are other free options, including Google Calendar. This is ideal because it's cloud-based, meaning you can access it from anywhere with any device. You should always use a calendar that is cloud-based; otherwise, you'll spend all your time trying to sync and update all your diary entries on different devices. With the cloud, it's done as soon as you enter the event/task, and you don't risk losing it.

Evernote

Evernote is my best friend in the cloud. I'm not talking about an imaginary friend who sits on a cloud talking to me every now and again (now, that would make me a little strange, wouldn't it?). I'm taking about an app – and it's an absolute lifesaver. Most of my best ideas come to me from nowhere, usually when I'm in the shower or driving. If it wasn't for Evernote, I would lose or forget them all.

Before Evernote, whenever an idea came into my head I used to try and remember it until I got a chance to write it down. It never worked. I'd sit at my laptop trying to rack my brain about what it was, but it would never come back to me. It was lost in the ether, never to be found again. Then I discovered Evernote – this fabulous little app that allows you to write notes wherever you are. It sits in the cloud so you can use it on any device – phone, tablet, computer, whatever. You make a note on your phone and it's there waiting for you when you sit down at your laptop. None of my ideas go missing, even if I'm driving (I pull over to make the note, of course!). When I'm lying in bed, and a thought starts bouncing around in my head, I pick up my phone and put it on Evernote. I couldn't sleep otherwise, so it also works as a relaxant.

Some of you might be thinking this is pretty basic, and good old-fashioned pen and paper would do the same. OK, but could pen and paper take a picture of text and automatically put that text into a note? Evernote (https://evernote.com/) is a super-clever little tool that keeps you organised and sharp, which is why it has over 100 million users, including me.

Dropbox

Dropbox allows you to keep and share documents in the cloud. Like Evernote, you can use it from any device. It's great for storing documents that require ongoing work (such as a project or when writing a book). You could start a document on your tablet, and continue writing it on your laptop. You can go to it at any time and add to it, knowing it will be updated and saved safely, even if you lose your device.

I've used other cloud storage services and lost work due to it not being saved. Dropbox has been consistently reliable, and also has a generous free storage allowance, meaning you can store and share lots of files for nothing. There will always be documents and files in your life you need to store safely. If your computer crashed right now, which files would you miss? Don't wait for a stress-inducing disaster: instead, save your files to Dropbox, immediately!

Download Dropbox free from www.carlvernon.com/resources.

TeamViewer

TeamViewer is a lovely bit of kit. It's a free service you can use to view a computer remotely. Let's say you forgot something on your work computer, and you're in dire need of it, or you have a project to complete and would prefer to do it sitting at home in front of the fire sipping a glass of wine rather than at your office desk. TeamViewer allows you to do exactly that. You just download it on your work computer (from www.teamviewer.com) and follow the instructions for how to add it to your home computer/laptop. Hey presto! Like magic you'll be able to access any computer you like from anywhere in the world – all you need is an internet connection. You can see why TeamViewer is perfect if you fancy having more flexibility and time away from the office. Maybe you'd prefer to complete your work project on a beach? (Although that probably defeats the object of being on a beach!)

If you choose to give TeamViewer a go, the novelty can tempt you into more work, but it shouldn't be used to increase your workload – its purpose is to give you mobility and the less-stress lifestyle we seek.

Avoid toxic people

One of the most effective ways of streamlining and de-stressing your life is to avoid toxic people. As well as a lot of good people, there are also a lot of horrible ones out there, so you can't – and shouldn't – embrace everyone.

A client of mine had a friend she had known from school (about 20 years in total). Religiously, they met every Saturday for a coffee and a catch up. Her friend had always demonstrated some behaviours of a toxic person, like making inappropriate comments and being negative about other people, but it was never enough for my client to pay close attention. That was until it became evident that her friend was doing everything behind her back to try and break up her relationship with her partner and other close friends (a classic trait of a toxic person). Because she was unhappy, she wanted her friend to get a taste of unhappiness (another trait). She wanted my client to herself, and was jealous of the fact her friend had a life outside of their weekly meet ups.

Toxic people rarely have enough going on in their own lives, so they create drama for everybody else – and drama is always waiting around the corner. They like to portray their lives are perfect (through narcissistic behaviour), but it's usually masking their unhappiness. If you're affected by a toxic person don't take it personally – it rarely is personal. It's just that you're one of the few putting up with their behaviour, so you tend to get the brunt of it.

Toxic people can be found in all forms of life. They could be a family member or even a close friend. You know the type I'm talking about – they never have a good word to say, and if they do say something, it's usually negative. If you're having a bad day, they somehow make it worse. Cut them out of your life as much as you can. It sounds a little harsh, I appreciate that, but these people are doing you no good. They are sinking, and they are happy to take down everything with them. They'll do it without a moment's thought. It's time you became a little more selfish. There are plenty of people out there with a similar mindset to you, and it's never been a better time to find them. When you surround yourself with people who have a positive outlook on life, people with drive and ambition, see how different your life becomes.

You are the result of your environment

It's also worth considering the law of attraction when deciding who you want in your life because we're all emotionally connected. It's essential that you surround yourself with people who have a positive influence on you and your life. It was only when I had the strength to stop allowing negative people in my life that I appreciated what an adverse influence they had on it. Some of my friends never had a good word to say about anybody, including me. Since I decided to keep them at a distance, I've felt much better. I admit that I needed help with this at first. I felt guilty for cutting people out of my life, even though they weren't any good for me. However, the guilt soon faded because (a) I had nothing to feel guilty about, and (b) I felt much better.

Try to avoid negative, cynical individuals who never have anything good to say; otherwise, you'll attract more of the same yourself. You'll inevitably meet such people, but try not to get sucked in. You have to be strong – and sometimes a little ruthless. If you keep letting them in your life, you *will* attract more negativity. I'm not saying cut everybody out of your life – far from it. Even the most happy-go-lucky individuals will have flaws and bad days. You know the people I'm talking about, though – the storytellers who have an excuse for everything; the emotional vampires who drain you of energy and joy. Keep them at arm's length, especially while establishing your less-stress lifestyle. You need as much positivity as you can get. Go looking for positivity, attract it, and you'll get as much as you want.

Chapter 16

Manage your environment

If your environment isn't right, every bit of advice in this book will be wasted. With the best will in the world, it can be incredibly difficult to fix what might be preventing you from growing if your environment is holding you back. It's a bit like keeping a flower in the dark – its potential is to flourish and be beautiful, but it will never reach that potential if it isn't getting the sunshine it needs.

Lots of people are being kept in the dark, and it's likely you are too. In this instance, the 'dark' might be a dead-end job, a bad relationship, a toxic friend, too much debt – it could be pretty much anything that's causing you negative thoughts. To move forward and create a less-stress lifestyle, you need to establish why you're allowing these things to keep you in the dark. The cause is usually related to two things: **people** and **you**.

People

People are your main source of great happiness and unhappiness. I'm talking about *everybody* – even the people closest to you. They will do incredible things for you, things you never expected, that bring you great joy and happiness. They'll also let you down when you don't expect them to, causing you sorrow and unhappiness. This is all part of taking the rough with the smooth – because you can't have one without the other. You have to accept both realities, but also realise there is a big difference between people letting you down and toxic people who are simply no good for you.

Toxic people keep you in the dark. They are the ones telling you why you shouldn't do something because you're only going to fail anyway. They are constantly reinforcing the fact that failure is waiting around the corner, and telling you that you shouldn't do something because it doesn't fit in with what's 'normal'. *That doesn't fit in with what I think is acceptable, so I'm going to tell you what a bad idea it is.*

The hardest thing that the big achievers and less-stress livers have had to overcome is negativity from other people (toxic and otherwise). Overcoming what the doubters have to say and not being sucked in with 'the norm' is one of the most difficult challenges we'll ever face. If you think about it, the only way to achieve more than the average is to be different from the average. If you were the same as everybody else (the same people who are telling you it's a bad idea), you'd be doing the same as they are. And what are they doing? Being the same as everybody else – overworked, overstressed and generally miserable.

Listen to yourself above anybody else. You dictate your environment, not somebody else. It's up to you to shape your environment; otherwise, someone else will. If you keep listening to – and believing – what everybody else thinks is right for you, you'll never get anywhere. Only you know what is right for you, and if it's different to what's right for everybody else, that can only be a good thing! You want to be different. You don't want to be overworked, overstressed and miserable. I know this because you've picked up this book.

You've picked up this book because you're different. You know that something else exists. You know that life has more to offer than the life you're living. You know that a life that isn't filled with stress and constant anxiety about the future is achievable, even if your environment might not be telling you so. Stick with me, because you're absolutely right.

Everybody will have negative episodes – it's impossible to stay positive 100% of the time. Even the happiest and most positive people have bad days. Should you cut these people out of your life for having a bad day? Of course not. You know the type of toxic people I'm talking about. I mentioned them in the last chapter. They are the ones who never have anything positive to say. They are life's victims, destined always to stay the same. You have to be strong and limit the time you spend with these people. I say 'strong' because they could be somebody very close to you – people you think you should give unconditional love and attention to. This is rubbish! These people are bringing you down, and you must lay down your own ground rules – one being that, unless they can support you on your journey to become a better you, you have no time for them. As I say, you have to be strong and this isn't easy, but you'll feel 100% better when you surround yourself with positive people.

Cut the toxicity from your life, and you'll flourish.

You

The most important thing keeping you in the dark and away from the sunshine is *you*. You're the only person you *really* need to convince, and you're the only person left to convince. There are no excuses apart from those you're creating. You're making up all your limiting beliefs, and they're all lies! These limiting beliefs are seriously holding you back, so I want you to ask yourself a couple of questions: **Why not me? Why shouldn't I be allowed to change my life?**

Good questions, right? Why not you? Are you not as deserving as anybody else on the planet? I can give you countless examples of people who have achieved great happiness and freedom. Are these people more deserving than you? I doubt it. Why not you?

Even if you achieve your goals (the same goals you told yourself were impossible), plenty of people have achieved the same goals – or beaten them. People are doing what you perceive to be impossible every day; it's just that their belief systems are different to yours. When they set out to create more happiness and less stress (to build a less-stress lifestyle), they also started out beating themselves up with negative thoughts and limiting beliefs (we all do – it's part of the process), but at least they made a start.

When they reached their goal, as well as reaping the rewards of being happier and less stressed, they looked back and wondered what all the fuss was about. It completely changed their belief system, and now, rather than saying things can't be done, they say: *If that was possible, what else is?* It's this type of curiosity that has allowed you to switch on a light, call and speak to somebody on the other side of the world, Google an answer on the internet to any question, switch your TV on and watch your favourite movie, drive to your friend's house, and fly to visit a different part of the world within hours.

If you don't at least try and make a start, how are you ever going to know if the impossible is possible? How are you ever going to know if your goals are achievable? How are you ever going to know what it feels like to live a less-stress lifestyle?

The biggest breakthrough you will make is convincing yourself. As soon as you do that, everything beyond it is simple.

Smash your tank

If you put a fish in a tank, it grows to a comfortable size within that tank. This is similar to when you put a plant in a pot – it will only grow as big as the pot allows. Same with humans: we only grow as much as we're allowed to grow. This brings up the question: how big do you want your tank to be?

Unlike the fish or the plant, you have the opportunity to decide how big a tank you want. (Or you could be more like the fish and allow others to dictate how big your tank is.)

If you want to achieve a less-stress lifestyle you have to be prepared to smash your tank. In other words, be prepared to change your current thought patterns and expect massive personal growth in return (and be comfortable with that). Not everybody is comfortable with that because it presents new challenges – normally regarding going against the crowd.

Most people think they are ready to smash their tank, but when the process begins, or the dream becomes reality, they weren't as ready as they thought. They watch the crowd going in the opposite direction and find it hard not to join in with them. If you do this, your tank and its size are chosen for you, and if you don't fit in it, you'll get fired.

How long are you going to allow others to choose your tank for you? This is a crucial question when making a start in your less-stress lifestyle, because if you're happy with others dictating your life for you and you're not willing to take responsibility yourself it's never going to happen.

I'm not saying you should immediately quit your job (if you have one). At this stage, I'm just trying to open your mind a little to the fact that it's up to you how your future looks – not others.

(There are some plants that will outgrow their pots. Their roots will burst out of the sides and any opening they can find. Ambition will do that to you.)

ACTION 10:
MAKE YOUR MONEY WORK FOR YOU

Chapter 17

Who wants to be a millionaire?

Am I a millionaire? No. Do I want to be a millionaire? If it means being financially and emotionally free, yes, why not? If it means me working every hour under the sun and being owned by the very thing I thought was giving me freedom, then no thanks.

I've met enough millionaires to know their lives are not all perfect. Generally, they are not happy people. Not because of their wealth. (I would rather have a million in the bank than not, right?) Many people believe that the more money they have, the happier they will be. However, research shows this is far from the truth. Nobel prizewinning psychologist Daniel Kahneman surveyed 1000 Americans, and found that happiness did increase with a higher income, but only to a certain point. That point was about $75,000 (equivalent to about £60,000). Earning above this level did nothing to boost happiness. I understand the research, because when we know we can have whatever our hearts desire, there's nothing to chase any more, and when there's no chase we lack focus and purpose – two important ingredients needed for happiness.

If you're not happy, it doesn't matter how much money you have in the bank – it's as simple as that. Money alone will *not* make you happy.

Forget about the money

The mistake many people make is to look at happiness from a purely monetary viewpoint. To some people, £50,000 would make a massive difference to their lives, whereas others might need £1,000,000, or as little as £100. Therefore, it's not being a millionaire that is the real difference here – it's the lifestyle that money creates, and the difference it makes to your life. Being a 'millionaire' is insignificant to living a happy life. It's just a figure. Have a look at the stories below.

Sarah

Sarah is a project manager for a charity that supports vulnerable young children. She earns £25,000 a year and is married with two children aged eight and twelve. She starts and finishes work at the same time every day, and her job also gives her the flexibility to work from home every Friday. She gets lots of quality time to spend with her family, including most evenings and every weekend. When she isn't spending time with her family she has the energy and passion to do her hobbies, which include writing her blog and working on her idea for a new business selling products online.

Joanne

Joanne works as an investment banker in London and has just made her first million. She lives alone and doesn't have time for a family due to her work commitments. Working twelve hours a day, seven days a week, to maintain her lifestyle, she eats and sleeps when she can. The stress and pressure of her work are taking their toll, and she's started to experience chest pains. She ignores them and continues to work hard – because she doesn't know any other way.

- Is Sarah or Joanne most happy?
- Does Sarah or Joanne have the better quality of life?
- Is it Sarah or Joanne who is significantly shortening their lifespan for the sake of money?
- Does Sarah or Joanne have a better chance of creating, or sustaining, a less-stress lifestyle?

Being a 'millionaire' means nothing at all unless you have the time, passion, health and energy to enjoy it. (It's even better to enjoy it with other people.)

If the path to being a millionaire looks like this . . .

MISERY > MISERY > MISERY > MILLIONAIRE > BIT OF HAPPINESS > MISERY

. . . would you really want to follow that path?

The less-stress lifestyle path looks like this . . .

ENJOY THIS MOMENT > ENJOY THIS MOMENT > IT DOESN'T MATTER WHAT HAPPENS NEXT

What happens next doesn't matter – because it doesn't exist yet. Of course, it's important to pay attention to your goals and future, but life is about enjoying the journey as much as the destination. In other words, your goal is your destination, but if you're miserable and depressed getting there, is it worth it? If the answer is yes, keep going, but don't complain about being miserable – you're only torturing yourself and the people around you.

I like to make happiness and freedom my destination (goal). By doing so, the journey tends to result in a lot more happiness and freedom.

Enjoy this moment

If you're set on becoming a millionaire, like I was as a kid, I'd like you to ask yourself one question: why? The usual answers to this question are:

'So I can do what I like when I like.'
'So nobody can tell me what to do.'
'So I can be free.'

You can do all the above without being a millionaire, and without working yourself to death to make it happen. You can start enjoying today, rather than thinking you can enjoy your life a little later down the line – when it happens. The 'when it happens' mentality is a tease. It's another way of you preventing yourself from enjoying life. Plus, it may never happen. The only thing that is real is this moment, right now, so you'd better start enjoying it, otherwise you'll never be happy, no matter what happens.

I had to work hard to break the 'when this happens, I'll be happy' pattern. Because I put great expectations on certain things making me happy, like sports cars and designer clothes, it ended up with me being disappointed and disillusioned. I worked myself into the ground to make these things happen, and in the end they didn't. This is why happiness is a journey, not a destination. Of course, the plane ride isn't as nice as the cocktail on the beach, but the cocktail hasn't been poured until you get there.

The greatest trick for happiness lies in enjoying the journey just as much as the destination. I suppose the biggest question is: how? How do you enjoy a plane ride as much as sipping a cocktail on a beach? Unfortunately, I can't give you the magic answer, and it's something I'm still working on every day – but I'm slowly getting better at it, with practice. The start of me allowing this process to happen is appreciating this moment, right now: appreciating that this moment is the only thing that exists, and not worrying about what may or may not happen. I'll put my headphones in and listen to an audio book, rather than sit and worry about things that don't exist. Usually, before I know it, the plane is ready to land, and I'm closer to enjoying my cocktail.

Start enjoying this moment and living now – it really is the only way to be happy.

Give money purpose

Although being a millionaire isn't the end goal, we still need to look at money, including how much you need to achieve a less-stress lifestyle: in other words, how much you need to earn to fulfil your goals – and no more. You simply don't need any more than that, and if you strive for it, you're only punishing yourself with more unnecessary working hours and stress.

If you have children or grandchildren, the money required to achieve your goals will extend past your own needs (because if you want to leave something behind, you have other people to think about). This brings up the question, 'how much do I need?' There is no definite answer to this, but most people will want to earn enough to give their children a university fund and perhaps to help them on to the property ladder. This is more than most children receive (certainly a lot more than I got!), but I'd hope the strategies you adopt from this book will allow you to fulfil your goals as well as your children's.

Another way of thinking about how much money you need is to understand what you want. The easiest way to do this is to set some goals, place a monetary value on them, work out what you need to do to achieve them (the sacrifice), and what it will mean to you once you have it (the reward). You can then decide whether or not it's worth your time and effort (the outcome).

Let's have a look at two examples that use two of my clients.

Paul

Goal: Paul wanted a Porsche 911 Carrera – a car he had admired since he was a boy.

Money: £86,000/deposit £21,000/monthly payments of £900

Sacrifice: He had to earn enough for the deposit and make sure he could cover payments for 36 months.

Reward: He got to fulfil a childhood dream and drive one of the most beautiful – and admired – machines on the road and enjoy the driving experience.

Outcome: We discussed his options and affordability, and decided to defer this goal until he could comfortably afford it using passive income (see Chapter 17). The decision was based on the large deposit being dead money (paying for depreciation) and the stress it would cause him to meet the high monthly payments and maintenance costs over three years. The car would be an absolute luxury, and other things must take priority.

Jen

Goal: Jen wanted another buy-to-let property to add to her passive income.

Money: Property cost £165,000/deposit £41,250/ monthly mortgage payments of £348

Sacrifice: She would use a significant amount of her savings and available capital, and would have to put a hold on other luxuries.

Reward: The property becomes part of her passive income portfolio (see Chapter 17), giving her a monthly income while appreciating in value.[1]

Outcome: Jen bought the house and it appreciated by £15,000 within six months. The profit she receives on rental income (£400 a month after costs) goes towards her less-stress lifestyle.

I know that getting your hands on such a high deposit to buy a house is difficult, but it's worth noting that Jen was flat broke just three years ago. She now has three properties (this one was her third). She did it by adopting the strategies in this book.

---

[1] *In the short term, property doesn't always increase in value. However, over time, evidence proves that it does – as long as you can afford to cover the dips in the market.*

It's worth you spending some time figuring out your goals and writing them down. List them as I have above, starting with the goal, the money you need up front and then each month, the sacrifice, the reward, and the outcome.

- What is your goal?
- How much will it take to achieve your goal?
- Is it worth the sacrifice and stress?

If it all stacks up, make it happen.

Moderate or be miserable

Have you noticed we all want what we can't have – and when we do get it, we don't want it as much? This is not the case with everything, of course, but it is very common. That's why you can have too much of a good thing, and why moderation is important – it keeps things alive and more joyous. The same goes for money. If you have plenty of money, it brings you no joy: there's no fight any more, no passion. This is understandable – if you know you can buy anything you want, where's the real joy in making a purchase, compared to the pleasure you get from knowing you've really earned something?

If you're currently struggling to pay the bills and get by (and I've been there), you're probably reading this thinking it's rubbish. I can understand that, because I agree that having money is better than not having money. That isn't up for debate. The point I'm making here is moderation, even if it doesn't apply to you yet.

If you go all out to create too much of something, be prepared for it to make you miserable, including money. That's what makes the less-stress lifestyle perfect. Your goal isn't to create an excess of money – your goal is to create a lifestyle that makes you happy, while making the money you *need*. If this strategy creates a bit of extra wealth, make sure you get the balance right. Invest and secure your future (to provide peace of mind, and therefore less stress), but don't be greedy. You don't need to be.

If you find yourself with too much money and time (well done!), give it away. Donate to causes you believe in. Volunteer. This will make you much happier than just chasing the next paid-for happiness fix.

Debt

Managing debt correctly depends very much on your personality. If you're like me, you don't like a lot of debt because it becomes part of your negative emotional attachments, and therefore weighs heavy on your mind and increases your stress levels. If you don't mind having debt, again, this is OK, as long as you're handling it correctly.

Handled correctly, debt isn't a bad thing. It's just that most of us (including me, for a long period of my life) don't know how to manage it, and therefore it becomes a big problem for lots of people. It's very easy to get into debt nowadays, thanks to the government and banks. Since the 2008 global recession, banks have clamped down on it more, but you can still get a loan at a very low rate (at the time of writing, banks are offering loans at 3%). This is both good and bad. Good, because going into debt (which you can repay) can help you achieve your goals. Bad, because you saw what happened with the recession, including many people losing their homes.

It's way too easy just to pull out the plastic when going shopping – this is an example of bad debt, and how not to manage it. It's also easy to go out and get a loan for the car you've always wanted. If you haven't got the money now, why wait? Get a loan! Yes . . . and no! Let's go back to Chapter 5: 'Can you *really* afford it?' I'm not just talking about the monthly loan repayment – I'm talking about your future as a whole. Yes, you get the car you've always wanted without having the cash up front, but what is the debt doing for you? Is it helping you grow and achieve your goals? In this instance, I doubt it. This is pointless debt – debt that is only going to weigh you down and ultimately limit your growth.

Debt is productive when it helps move you forward. Most of us wouldn't be able to afford a home without a mortgage. I wouldn't have been able to acquire my investment properties if I hadn't taken out loans on them. The difference between these things and a car bought with debt is the properties help me move my life forward and achieve a less-stress lifestyle. Buying a car with a loan and using a credit card when shopping doesn't. These are luxuries, and should be treated as such – otherwise you'll find yourself with lots of debt and very little to show for it.

I'm not saying you shouldn't treat yourself – of course you should! Life would be pretty dull without treats. Just buy them when you can *really* afford them. I don't mean you should wait until you've saved £30,000 so you can pay for the car in cash – again, that is a bad strategy for a number of reasons, including: (1) you wouldn't want to put all your capital into something that rapidly depreciates, and (2) if you wait to save £30,000, you'll probably be waiting a long time! Build your passive income first, and then buy your luxuries and toys later, with debt you *can* afford – debt you can spread as a monthly payment with a nice low rate. This is another reason why putting things on your credit card is not a good idea – such purchases often come with really high rates, and even if the initial rate is low, it won't last for long, so you'll find yourself paying for it later. Banks offer a nice rate at the start to entice you in – because they know they'll get you eventually! One possibility is continually transferring your credit card balance to a new 0% deal when your previous one expires. I do this. I have a moderate balance I continually transfer when my deal comes up for renewal, usually every two to three years. All I pay for the privilege is a small transfer fee each time. If you follow suit, be mindful of two things: (1) make sure you keep track of when your deal is up for renewal so you can transfer it in good time and prevent yourself from paying high interest once your deal is up, and (2) to get the best 0% deals with low balance transfer fees, you need a good credit history.

Learning to move debt and manage it correctly with strategies like the 0% credit deal will massively reduce your stress and make you feel much more free and happy. Again, I speak from experience. In my early twenties I was £50,000+ in debt, with very little to show for it. Everything I'd bought (including my car) had depreciated, and I was heavily in negative equity. It was one of the most stressful and depressing times in my life. Ironically, to try and compensate for how bad I felt, I'd buy more things, which just put me in more debt! This became a vicious cycle that was very hard to break.

Eventually, I managed to break the cycle by deciding to invest in myself and learning how to use debt wisely. With a bit of hard work, and after time, generating a passive income allowed me to pay off most of my debt within a few years, while also enjoying life's luxuries.

Chapter 18

Make your money work for you

You already know that if you make money your focus, you will struggle to find happiness. However, money is very much a fixed part of our lives, and it's a struggle to live a less-stress lifestyle without it (unless you want to go and live in the woods, foraging for berries and living in a den).

Assuming you'd rather live in luxury, you're going to need an income. That doesn't mean that you have to work hard for the money. In fact, you can arrange it so your money works for you – that's the less-stress lifestyle way.

Passive income

If you're not familiar with the term 'passive income', it's basically income received on a regular basis with little (or no) effort required to maintain it. Sounds fantastic, doesn't it? Well, it is. It's your key to a less-stress lifestyle and your way out of the rat race – so this chapter will tell you how to achieve it.

Passive income is a way of getting money to work for you, rather than the other way around. It's the savviest form of income there is, and you absolutely need to know more.

This chapter will cover different ways to generate passive income, but I thought I'd give you a quick example to prove its worth. When building a business it's normal to look at staff as the income generator, but staff can be one of the biggest forms of stress. Managing them takes up all your time, and you are constantly responsible for them. Instead, let's say you focused on selling a book. A book is classed as passive income because once it's written and selling, you don't need to do anything else. If you have an agent and publisher, you don't need to manage it in any way. The same goes for a rental property. If you pay an agent to manage it for you, it provides you with an income, with no/very little effort required. Books and houses are your new employees – without the stress and responsibility. They become your assets, which allow you to live your less-stress lifestyle. Welcome to the world of passive income!

If you weren't familiar with passive income before reading this, I'm sure it's continuing to sound like a dream. It is, but one that can be achieved. However, I'll start by saying that passive income is not easy to amass due to the time, effort and money it can take to build it to a successful level. But knowing that it exists is the first step in making it happen. Believe me, there are plenty of people out there who know all about it, and are reaping its rewards.

Most days, I go to the gym at about 10am. I do this because I find I have a good amount of energy at that time and it's quieter, so I get to use the equipment I want at my leisure. However, I've noticed over the years it's gradually got busier. Why aren't these people at work? I used to wonder. Listening to their conversations (I'm nosey), and watching them, I discovered the answer.

Putting aside inheritance, retirement and lottery winners, there are increasing numbers of people discovering the magic of passive income – people who go to the gym at 10am rather than 6am, because they can; people who spend a Friday afternoon with their children rather than stuck behind a desk at work, because they can; people who can take a longer lunch, knowing their boss isn't waiting to breathe down their neck, because they can. They're doing all these privileged things because **money is working for them**, not the other way around. This is what passive income does for you.

I do all of these things. I do them knowing that my passive income sources are working for me, even when I'm at the gym, or taking my daughter to the park, or ordering an extra drink at lunch. As I said, it's not easy, and it took me years of hard work to achieve it, but because I decided to focus on passive income and put my strategy into action, I'm reaping the rewards today. I've had to make sacrifices to make it happen – such as writing in the evening rather than watching television – but it's all part of the immediate sacrifice for the long-term good.

Types of passive income

Before we move forward, it's worth noting (again) that creating passive income is hard work, takes time, and doesn't happen overnight. But here's another way of looking at it: if you're currently already working hard, why not put more effort into building a passive income?

I wish I had a magic wand and was able to give you an exact strategy for your passive income, but the truth is, everybody's route to freedom is going to be different. I make no bones about the fact that it takes hard work to achieve it, no matter how smart you are – but, as stated previously, it's well worth the effort.

It's completely up to you whether you decide to build your passive income in one way, or through five ways, or whether you look to develop a product, write a book, start a blog or buy property. Just don't forget what the aim is here – to produce a passive income to achieve your goal of a less-stress lifestyle, with as little effort required as possible.

Intellectual property (books/ideas)

To write a successful book, you don't need to reinvent the wheel or come up with a unique idea. Some best-selling books are based on other people's stories – stories that inspire and are worth writing about. You don't need a personal story – you just need enough passion and enthusiasm to want to write about something that interests you (and will interest others). Saleability is, of course, a priority. There is little point writing a book if nobody is interested in reading it. To make your book saleable, it needs to get people's attention and have a USP (unique selling point) – to distinguish it from all the others available.

If you write about a specific subject, a lot of the book could be made up of interviews with experts in that field. When you contact them, you might find that most experts will be more than happy to help a budding writer. The desire to help others is within all of us, so take advantage of it. They might ask to be paid – or you might be lucky and ask somebody who is happy just getting the exposure. You'll never know until you ask! If they do want something in return, give them an incentive. If you don't have any money, negotiate a deal with them where you'll give them a cut of sales. If you're going to succeed, you have to get creative. Combine your creativity with the will to succeed, and things will happen for you.

Unless you're a best-selling author (I'm talking like Stephen King or J. K. Rowling), selling books alone won't be enough to sustain a comfortable lifestyle – you need to know that before you grab your laptop and start tapping away. Have you ever met an author driving around in a Ferrari? No, me neither. The mental picture you have of a writer being a scruffy-looking recluse in their dressing gown is generally accurate – apart from me, of course!

Because writing a book is such a competitive space, it's treated as such. It's very much viewed as a privilege to get a publishing deal, which is why royalties are low. Books are a good way to get noticed and reach a wide audience (meaning they can form a strong part of your overall strategy), but they won't support your less-stress lifestyle alone. Once you have your audience, you can add value to the time invested in writing by doing things like workshops and coaching. However, writing a book alone doesn't guarantee attention. Unless you're an established big name it's very difficult for authors to get noticed, even if a world-leading publisher signs you up.

Based on the odds, writing books is a high-risk strategy. In 2013 China published 440,000 books, the USA 305,000, and the UK 184,000. That's a lot! It seems as though it's most people's ambition to write a book, making it a very competitive market. And getting published is just the start. A common misconception about publishers is that they sell your books for you – they don't! Yes, the bigger ones have sales, marketing and PR teams, but ultimately it's up to you to sell your books.

I write because I enjoy it, and I get huge satisfaction from helping people through my writing. I'm also not afraid to take a gamble if I believe in something. I'd recommend you write (if you're going to) for the same reasons: enjoyment and wanting to help – not for money.

I appreciate I've been quite negative here, but I'm being realistic about the odds. You can, of course, make your fortune by coming up with the next Harry Potter series, but the fact remains that there are lots of authors out there. Plus, writing is hard! (Well, it is for me!) Writing a decent book is very time-consuming and isn't an easy job (which is probably why there are so many rubbish ones available). The number of times I go through each paragraph to make sure it's right (I'm a perfectionist) is excruciating at times. But I remind myself of how many people I can help, and I carry on. It's my passion for writing that makes all the difference for me, and it will make the difference for you, too.

If you do have a passion for writing and want to try to beat the odds, there are generally two options when deciding to write a book: (1) self-publish, and (2) write with the aim of finding an agent and getting published. More and more authors are going down the self-publishing route because it's never been easier. Remember, a book is just a product like any other – if you believe you can sell it, you're in business. You can be your own publisher as long as you have what it takes to sell your book.

Because the self-publishing route takes a lot of effort and time, my advice is to focus on getting published first, and if it doesn't happen within a timescale suited to you, go down the self-publishing route. Don't be disheartened if it doesn't happen overnight. It's incredibly competitive, and most books don't get a deal with a publisher. Even some of the best authors were rejected time and time again!

Like anything else, if you have a passion for writing and an absolute belief that you can make it happen, it will.

Licensing

Similar to books, you don't necessarily need to reinvent the wheel when it comes to products. You can either invent a product to license out, or license an existing product to sell (both options qualify as passive income).

If you have a great idea, you can license it out to somebody (a company) that already has the audience for that product. For example, if you invent a new genius way of your car finding a parking spot for you (if you do, please get in touch and let me know!), you would do better approaching the major car manufacturers directly and licensing it to them, rather than trying to invent an entire new car to fit around that product. They would pay you a licence fee, potentially for every sale, and all you would need to do is sit back and wait for your cheque in the post. This is as good as passive income gets. This strategy is also perfect for your focus – your only target audience is buyers at the car manufacturer, rather than the entire car driving market. The more focused your pitch is, the more likely you are to succeed.

On the other side of licensing, you can be the licensee. You can take somebody else's idea/product and sell it yourself. There's not as much money in this, though, and if you're competing with other resellers, it can get very competitive. In this instance, things tend to come down to price, so it can take the challenge and enjoyment out of it. If it only comes down to price, you can guarantee there will always be somebody willing to sell at a lower margin than you. You can safeguard against this by negotiating an exclusive deal, but you'll need to demonstrate to the product owner that you are the best person to sell the product. If they're willing to give the product to you, and you demonstrate little in the way of selling ability, the product is probably poor, so you wouldn't want to waste your time and energy on it. If something is worth having, it usually means fighting for it.

Finding a product to license is easier than you might think – as easy as contacting the product owner and asking them if you can sell their product. Maybe you've used a product and like it. Maybe you used it in another country, and think it could do well in your homeland.

www.licensingexpo.com is a worldwide exhibition with product owners demonstrating to potential licensees. With a bit of research, you'll find other exhibitions local to you. There are some big opportunities out there if you're willing to take the time to look.

Blogs

You have to make it pretty big to earn money from a blog alone. Blogs earn money from affiliate marketing (selling other companies' products on your website, and referring customers to their website). If you want to sell high-end products on your site, you need to have a high enough visitor hit-rate to get them interested. To encourage more visitors to your blog you need to offer something that people need and want, including quality content.

The problem with writing a blog that has quality content (it has to be good quality, otherwise, people will dismiss it and never visit again) is that it's very time-consuming. Again, because anybody can write a blog, there are thousands of blogs out there on the same subjects, making it a competitive space. However, a good blog can give you great exposure, sometimes very quickly. If a blog post or video goes viral it can reach millions of people within days – there are very few things that offer that level of exposure.

To make it big in the area you choose, you have to show people you know what you're talking about. They will have to feel comfortable with you and the advice you're offering.

Nowadays, bloggers, vloggers, YouTubers and Instagrammers are also celebrities. If a company, say a fashion company, is looking to launch a new brand, they will turn to these guys to help them. Top bloggers have a strong and loyal following, and their audience tends to listen to them. If they say a product is worth a purchase, it can make the company's sales rocket overnight.

If you decide to start blogging, I recommend setting up an email subscription allowing visitors to sign up to your newsletter, which will help you draw, and keep, an audience. I use MailChimp to automate the email subscription process. I find it to be more professional than most of the other email delivery providers, with a better rate of success (that is, emails not going into spam folders).

If you're looking for a blogging platform, I recommend WordPress. If you're looking for more of an e-commerce website with a blog attached to it, I recommend Weebly. Both offer lots of modern designs and are easy to use – you don't need to be a web designer to operate them. They have a drag and drop design function, which makes using their platforms very easy.

Like anything else, a blog/website has to start somewhere. If you're starting from scratch, it can be quite daunting looking at a blank canvas and the follower figure set at 0. For now, don't worry about that, just keep writing. The blank space will quickly fill, and your follower count will rise! The top blogs in the world (which have millions of visitors per week) all started in the same way.

Start using Weebly free from my website www.carlvernon.com/resources.

Post videos on YouTube

Online content via blogging is seriously overcrowded, which is why lots of people are turning their attention to 'vlogging' (video blogging). Plus, people are busy, so often they would much rather watch a few quick video posts than read a long blog post.

Like blogging, vlogging can give you a huge reach. We've all seen those cute cat videos which have hundreds of millions of views. If your video goes viral, you can achieve overnight success and celebrity status (if that's what you want). What I like best about vlogging is that you can do it quickly. You can do a short video within minutes; compare that to a blog post, which will take hours to write, read and reread for mistakes. Vlogging is not for the shy, but that's what will give you an advantage – the fact that not everybody wants to do it. Anybody can write a blog, but not everybody wants to put their mug on camera! It's worthwhile practising and getting good at it. When you're used to the process, you'll be able to do a vlog in minutes.

Coming back to the point of passive income, you can gain a small amount of advertising revenue through vlogging on YouTube, but it is tiny, and only really counts if you have millions of views. The best strategy for vlogging is to support another form of passive income by offering 'expert' advice on the subject. If you're looking to sell your new invention (a toilet roll holder that sits on your head), you can vlog about toilet roll holders and why having it sit on your head offers your audience the convenience of never running out. It's an indirect way of advertising: you're offering an advert your audience is much more likely to watch, compared to an actual advert. I'd watch it!

Online courses

One of the hardest forms of passive income is developing an online course. This takes a lot of work – and expertise – but can help you build a passive income.

A platform like Udemy has approximately seven million students looking for courses, and it can put you in touch with a big audience instantly.

You have to put in a lot of work to develop your online course, because it has to be good. If it isn't, there is no way people will pay for it. The internet is full of free stuff, so you need to demonstrate why your audience should pay for yours. To answer this question, ask yourself some questions:

- Would I pay for it?
- Why?
- What can I offer that isn't already available?
- How can I make it so the customer feels good about buying the course?
- How can I ensure that when they've completed it, they feel like it was value for money?

Do you have a skill others need/want? Can you learn a skill and reteach it? People will, of course, be more interested if you can demonstrate you have years of practical experience in your chosen field, but if you're engaging and professional, there isn't a skill you can't pick up and reteach. Some of the popular skills required tend to be tech-focused, like online marketing, using social media and coding. As technology continues to advance, there won't be a shortage of people looking to learn these types of skills.

The hard work is front-loaded, because once it's recorded, it's done. You will, of course, need to put work into marketing and promoting it, but if you use a good enough platform (like Udemy) and describe the course well enough with specific and niche keywords (to separate yours from the others), your audience is ready and waiting.

Find a link to Udemy on my website: www.carlvernon.com/resources.

Renting

Renting is pretty simple, really. If you own something that somebody needs, but they either can't afford to buy it or don't want to buy it, you're in business.

There is a bit of work to be done, depending on what you're renting, so you have to evaluate time/effort. For example, if the product is large, you need to think about logistics – where will you store it? – and costs (how will you transport it?). If the product is rented out by the day, you will need to work out time and effort, including filling in the necessary paperwork and shipping, to evaluate if the work is worth it. If you get it right, renting can be a lucrative business, especially if you can automate the process as much as possible.

A friend of mine has a passion for photography, which has led to her buying some expensive kit. Every now and again she rents some of her equipment out for the day (including cameras). Within a year she has made back what she paid for the equipment, so the products have paid for themselves. She's planning to sell the equipment to upgrade, so any money she makes from the sale is 100% profit. That's a wise strategy in anybody's book!

Do you own something you can rent out, such as equipment for an expensive or specialist hobby? If so, you could start small and keep trading up. Maybe you want to think bigger and have multiple rents? Whatever you decide to do, just keep evaluating your time and effort against the reward, and make sure it's worth it. If it is, your rental empire might come sooner than you think.

Products

Offering a product, compared to offering a service, can offer a passive income, but you have to get the process right because they do entail ongoing work. If you're thinking of developing a product from scratch, first you need an idea, then you have to design it, then decide on how to make it, formulate a strategy to sell it, and then you've got to ship it. You can probably work out why I've never dealt with products! But that doesn't mean you can't make it work. The world is full of products, and there are big opportunities out there!

There are simpler ways to deal in products. You could buy products in bulk from, say, China, and sell them online through eBay and Amazon. However, this is only simpler in principle – it's more complicated when you find yourself spending most of your time shipping the products and dealing with returns, only to receive a small financial reward.

For this to sustain a less-stress lifestyle, you usually have to hit big numbers (due to low margins), and that can take up a lot of your time (which defeats the object). Employing somebody will eat up all your profit, so that's not an option either. You could aim for higher-value or niche products, which people will pay top dollar for, but, again, this strategy could be risky (if the market is saturated, say).

Based on the above, selling products on eBay and Amazon will rarely make you enough income to allow thoughts of retirement, unless it becomes a full-time thing (which isn't the goal of a less-stress lifestyle). However, it is an easy place to start, especially if you're looking to do something in addition to your current job. Most people don't want to take the great leap from a full-time job to nothing (and rightly so), and selling products on the side can offer the perfect transition. If you're not used to a bit of entrepreneurialism, selling products can give you the practice you need to continue to build your skill set and portfolio, allowing you to move on to bigger and better things.

Looking on the optimistic side, if you do invent a product, why can't it be the next big thing? If it is, you've cracked it – job done! If this happens, I'd love to hear about your success story.

Stocks and shares

I don't trade on the stock market. There are companies you can pay to trade for you, but since I'm a control freak, this wouldn't work for me either. It takes too long to learn to understand it, and it's a full-time commitment. I have the time, but not the patience. However, there are plenty of people making a lot of money trading on the stock market. It is risky – but, like all risk, the more you understand it, the less of a risk it is. If you're prepared to invest some serious time into getting your head around it, it might well become a significant part of your passive income.

I enjoyed the film *Wall Street*, but trading on the stock market doesn't always equate to driving around in limos while wearing braces and sucking on a cigar. If you decide to dabble in stocks, please do your homework. As a rookie, you can lose money a lot faster than make it. Remember, you have to keep your eye on your investments. You can set up automated systems to do the work for you, but ultimately it's up to you to research companies and make sure you're investing wisely.

Saving

Saving is the slowest and most tedious method of producing a passive income because of its minimal return. Nevertheless, every penny counts. Nowadays, you don't get much of a return for your money because saving interest rates are poor. Again, it's about risk and return. Saving offers the lowest risk, and therefore the lowest return. I would never recommend basing a passive income strategy on saving alone (unless you have millions to save), but to utilise it as part of your overall strategy if you want to.

The longer you're prepared to lock your money away in savings, the higher the rate. I'm not a fan of locking my money away for lengthy periods of time, and therefore the only savings account I utilise is usually an instant cash ISA. That's because I like instant access to my money, so when I'm ready, I can take it out and spend it on something that could offer a higher return, like property.

Peer-to-peer lending

Peer-to-peer lending carries a little more risk. If you haven't heard of peer-to-peer lending, it's basically people lending other people money. Rather than go down a traditional route (like getting a loan from a bank), you could use a peer-to-peer lending platform. The idea is you put in say, £100, along with fifty other people, and lend that money out to somebody who will use it for whatever purpose they need it for – a business, for example.

The return you get is higher than that you would receive with savings, but that's due to the risk involved (the person might not pay the debt back). This, of course, makes peer-to-peer lending riskier than savings, but it's up to you how much risk you're willing to take.

I wouldn't put all my money into peer-to-peer lending because – based on the above point – this would be a bad strategy. It could certainly be part of your passive income strategy because it fits the model well – once you release the funds, you don't have to do anything else: you just wait for the return on investment (ROI). If you're interested, start by Googling it, and do some research into who offers the best rates.

Be a silent partner (an angel investor)

For this example, think of the TV series *Dragons' Den*. If you've watched the programme, you'll know that people pitch their business ideas to the Dragons, who then decide whether or not to invest. The person pitching will have day-to-day responsibility for their business, and the

Dragons will put up their own cash for equity in that business, but will have no day-to-day responsibility for it. This makes the Dragons angel investors.

Being an angel investor requires you to have a lot of capital to invest, so it might be a longer-term strategy. If you currently have cash at your disposal, let's get into it . . .

Like with peer-to-peer lending, there are plenty of people wanting to borrow money. If you want to lend money and don't want day-to-day involvement in the business (this sounds exactly like what we're looking to achieve), being a silent partner offers the solution. As a silent partner that's all you do – give your money and let somebody else manage it.

You can do this in any industry, from property to pizza-making, and although you won't have any involvement in the business, it would help to have some interest in the subject/industry you're lending to. So, if you're a vegetarian, investing in a burger chain probably isn't your thing.

The risk here is the same as with peer-to-peer lending – you put money in and it's not paid back. The person(s) you lend it to could go bust and take your cash with them. This is one of the reasons why I would strongly advise not to lend your money to friends and family for their new ventures. It almost always ends up turning sour. If you want to lend money to friends and family, do it with the view that you are giving the money to them – this saves a lot of grief and potential rifts. With this in mind, it's probably best not to lend/give people money until you're in a position where you can afford it.

Due diligence is needed to become a successful angel investor, like any other investment. On a positive note (in this chapter I've been very cautious with my advice, and I hope it hasn't come across as negative), if you invest in the right company it can pay huge dividends. Imagine if you'd bought 25% of Google, Apple or Facebook in their fledgling days? Hello, less-stress lifestyle! There are some big and exciting opportunities out there!

If you decide to look into being an angel investor, there are plenty of platforms you can use that will put you in touch with people looking for investment. There are also regular events held for angel investors, and you can probably find one local to you. A good start is your local chamber of commerce or UK Business Angels Association (UKBAA): see www.ukbusinessangelsassociation.org.uk. These types of organisations operate in other countries under different names. If you Google 'business angels associations' you will find what you're looking for.

Do your research thoroughly, and don't jump in to something until you feel comfortable and know it's right for you.

Property

Most of my salary, bonuses, dividends and any other form of income I've received has gone into buying property. Property is a very expensive form of passive income, so I appreciate it's not a viable option for everybody, but if you do have capital at your disposal, it is one of the most powerful ways to create a less-stress lifestyle.

A typical buy-to-let deposit (at the time of writing) in the UK is 25%. That's a big chunk of capital which is not easy to acquire. Lots of workshops promise to teach you 'no money down' techniques to buy property (that means, not having to put down a deposit to buy a property), but I'm yet to see a genuinely sound investment that doesn't require a lump sum. However, there are lots of self-made property investors to draw inspiration from. Not everybody has been given money to invest, including me – I've had to work hard at making the money, and if you focus on achieving it, you can do the same. (If you do have a legal strategy for acquiring property without putting much money down up-front – one that doesn't require credit card funding – please get in touch. I'd love to share it with my readers.)

I own a small portfolio of properties in my local region. I find buying property in my local area a lower risk because I know the good areas (and the bad ones), and if a property needs my attention, it's easily accessible. I bought my first property when I was twenty (fifteen years ago) and I still rent it out today. In those fifteen years, I've rarely had any trouble with tenants, and only seen one significant property crash.

You should make up your own mind when it comes to how much risk you're comfortable with. I prefer to do my own homework, not depend on hearsay. I like to speak to other property developers and landlords. When I talk to them, I rarely hear horror stories. If I do, it's generally because tenants haven't been vetted properly, and the landlord has been sloppy. To reduce my risk and make my life as relaxed as possible, I use an agency that manages my properties for me. For a small fee, the agency takes care of everything, including vetting the tenants, and I only get involved if I need to.

I could write an entire book on property investment, but we've got plenty of other things to focus on. If you see property as one of your strategies for a less-stress lifestyle (and you should), my advice is to pick up some books on the subject. As soon as you're ready, concentrate on your local area (because you know it best), and don't be tempted to stray too far away (it will lead to more work). Speak to local agents and get them to do the legwork for you. I've never been to an auction, because they take too much time and effort, and there is a much higher risk that you might buy a money pit (auction properties can have issues like structural and legal problems, which is often why they're being sold at auction rather than on the open market). If you fancy diving straight in, go to one, and get a feel for it – just be prepared to take on a full-time project, as many auction properties require a lot of attention. With more and more people attending auctions, there are fewer bargains to be had, so I don't bother.

As I mentioned, don't forget what your ultimate aim is here – to produce a passive income with as little effort as possible. For me, that means buying property that needs a little work so I can add value to it, property that a good tenant would want to rent, and hiring an agent to look after it for me.

Building a strong and sustainable property portfolio takes time and effort (and lots of capital). It doesn't happen overnight. As I mentioned, anybody who tells you it does is usually offering something illegal, or wanting you to sign up to a seminar that offers bad advice. It's all about making a start. Set the pace by trying things like renting a commercial space, parking space, garage or spare room (Airbnb is worth a look). That's not for everybody, but you have to start somewhere, right?

Buy an existing business

So far, I've listed a lot of stuff that requires groundwork, but if you're lucky enough to have lots of capital behind you there is always the option to buy a business that is already earning a passive income. That's a win–win! You don't necessarily need a lot of capital – if the business is worth buying, you could get a loan. I say 'if the business is worth buying' because there are a lot that aren't! You also need to factor in the cost of the loan. Plus, if you borrow from a bank, they like to see that you possess experience in the field you're looking to purchase in, and if you haven't, they are less keen to give you money. This makes finding a new business difficult unless you have the capital yourself.

I have mixed views about franchises. If you don't know what a franchise is, Subway and McDonald's are two of the biggest, best-known examples. For a fee, Subway and McDonald's will let you trade under their brand names and will set you up with a complete business model. They will provide everything you need, and all you have to do is hire staff. Franchises never appealed to me because I have never liked the idea of being dictated to. Plus, you still have the headache of employing staff, whether you're Subway or Steve's Subs. There are obvious benefits to franchising, like having everything set up for you, and if you're looking to buy a business, they are worth considering. Again, it very much depends on what you're looking to get out of it. If you want control and the option to build your own brand, franchising isn't for you, but if you just want to put your money into something that already works, and you don't care about anything else, it could well be for you. The latter certainly falls more in line with a passive income strategy.

Only you know what's right for you. Initially, it pays not to be too fussy, because you might never find what you're looking for. A perfect business doesn't exist, but if it has enough potential, you can always change it to your preference once it's yours. If you can inject a healthy dose of passion, along with the will to succeed, you can make anything work.

Solve a problem

When looking for a new venture it's easy to overcomplicate things, but the truth is it's very straightforward. A successful venture comes down to one thing: **solving problems**. The bigger the problem, the more you get paid.

People will pay handsomely for convenience and to have their problems solved, and that's what industry is built on. When you leave your house today you'll buy lunch (solving the problem of hunger), you might buy petrol for your car (solving the problem of getting home), and a bunch of flowers (doing your best to solve the problem of the argument you had last night!).

Think about why you buy something, and why somebody else would buy from you, whether it's a product or a service. There are endless problems to solve, and that really is the place to start when looking for a new venture. Aim to serve – and you will never lose.

Networking

If you don't know where to go next, a networking event could be the solution you're looking for. Other people have a knack of stimulating ideas in you and, at a networking event, you'll meet other like-minded people willing to share information and ideas. If you see other entrepreneurs in action, it makes it all feel more real, and if you haven't taken the leap yet, they might provide the inspiration you need. Networking is also ideal if you're looking to form or find partnerships.

There will probably be several networking events in your local area – you just have to hit the internet and have a look (www.meetup.com could be a good start). Some are free and some you have to pay to join, although fees are usually minimal and worth the cost. Aim to go to four or five and get a feel for the ones you like – stick with them and continue to develop relationships. You never know where it could take you.

Meeting new people is the aim of the game here. If you want to live a certain type of lifestyle, you're better off meeting people who are already in that lifestyle. If you want to be a millionaire, hang out with them. Remember, you are the result of your environment, and if you want to *have*, you have to *be*. In other words, if you want to be a millionaire, start acting like one. Don't wait until you become one; start acting like one today. Start hanging around with millionaires and learn from them. This method is a real timesaver too, because it might turn out you don't want to be one after all.

Top golf clubs are a good place to start. Membership is pricey, sure, but just imagine the return on investment if you make friends with the right people who can make things happen for you. What if you don't play or like golf? Is that the point? No. If it means taking your life to the next level, get to like it! There are a lot worse things out there than playing a round of golf, believe me.

Other stomping grounds for high-performers tend to be expensive gyms and anything to do with aviation and boating. Events and shows for these things offer an excellent opportunity to rub shoulders with the super-successful. Learn from them. Watch how they act. Ask them questions, and get chatting. Is it intimidating? Only as much as you make it.

Meeting winners and high achievers by networking has expanded my mind to things I never thought possible. I'd recommend you do the same. The rewards could be huge.

Important note

These ideas are based on the things I know about and that have worked for me. There are many more ways to achieve a passive income, and lots of opportunities out there. The things that have worked for me might not work for you (and vice versa). I am not giving you personal financial advice. If you feel you need financial advice, or other expert assistance, you should seek the advice of a professional advisor.

My intention here is to get the creative side of your brain working, because the more creative you get, the better. If you can find something nobody else is doing and it works for you, you'll add instant value and improve your odds of long-term success.

This book and these ideas aren't necessarily about replicating other people's ideas – it's about expanding your mind so you can see and utilise more opportunities. Get researching, get creative, make a start – and, most importantly, have fun!

NOW IT'S TIME TO WIN
THE GAME . . .

Chapter 19

Win the game

Now you know the ten actions you need to take to create your new less-stress lifestyle, you're all set. However, self-motivation is sometimes hard to maintain, and falling back into bad old habits is way too easy, so here are some bonus chapters that will help you sustain the lifestyle you're about to build.

If you remember, in Chapter 6, 'The happiness trick', I mentioned why I like to view life as a game. As in any game, it helps to have winning strategies based on things that have worked in the past and have worked for others – things that keep you one step ahead in the fight to maintain freedom and happiness.

Here are some key game-winning strategies that have taken me years to develop and understand. They have made all the difference in helping me achieve and sustain a less-stress lifestyle.

Do what's *not* expected

I've always found that, when I go the extra mile by doing something that wasn't asked of me or expected, I tend to win.

I make an effort to do what's not expected in everything I do. For example, when somebody books on to one of my workshops, I send them a signed copy of my book with a personal message inside it. They also receive unexpected follow-ups from me, and it's these little touches that make all the difference.

If somebody expects something from you, it takes the surprise away from it. If you bought your partner a present every day, they would expect a present every day. If they didn't receive the present, they would be disappointed. Assuming you don't do this, when you do buy your partner a gift, it's treated as a pleasant unexpected surprise, and you get a lot more brownie points! This works best if you buy the gift on a random day, not their birthday – again, under these circumstances it's treated as the norm, and therefore less of a surprise. If you want to make your partner really happy, buy them a gift when they least expect it.

Going the extra mile and doing what's not expected takes time and effort, which is why it's important to choose things in life you want, so the time and effort you invest is worth it.

When I analysed some of the things I was putting effort into using the 80/20 principle, I noticed there was a lot of stuff I didn't really want to do, which was reflected in my quality of life and work. Doing things I didn't want to do demotivated me, and I had less desire to put any effort in. This did not improve my life, and seriously affected my happiness.

You can only put in the extra effort and do what's not expected when you're really into something, and that's the only way you're really going to win big. We can all go and win a mediocre client because the reward is usually mediocre. It takes passion and going the extra mile to win something that is really worth winning. It takes the ability to deliver something that wasn't expected.

If you want to find a partner (one you find mentally and physically attractive, who challenges you, and who loves you as much as you love them), you have to do what's *not* expected.

If you're looking to elevate your business to the next level, you have to do what's *not* expected.

If you're looking to break the monotony of your average life, you have to do what's *not* expected.

Break the pattern and keep doing things that nobody else is doing, and watch your life change. Just make sure you're doing things that are worth your time and effort – the things that make you want to do what's not expected.

Think ABC (Always Be Closing)

If you want to create a less-stress lifestyle and get on in life, you have to be good at selling. You have to know how to close a deal. I expect readers will have one of two reactions to this:

1: Oh, great . . . I love selling. I'm a natural salesperson and have no problem with this.
2: Oh, great . . . that's me up s#it creek without a paddle.

This bit isn't just for the number 2s. Everybody will benefit from being able to sell better, because it creates 'good' stress in your life – the type of stress we're after to achieve our goals. Plus, you will *not* get where you want to be if you're no good at selling. If you think you'll just get other people to sell for you, I'm afraid that won't work either. You have to be able to convince and influence others. In other words, you need the ability to sell yourself.

Whether you like it or not, you are constantly selling. Work colleagues, friends, siblings and spouses all get a daily dose of what you're 'selling'. Getting your child to go to bed and asking your friend for a lift are a couple of examples.

You can write the best book in the world, but if you can't sell, it won't get past the office junior, who will just put it in the reject pile because you don't have a PhD.

Before you start thinking that selling is beneath you, it might surprise you to learn that the best salespeople on the planet aren't selling cars or gold watches. They are running countries (Barack Obama and Vladimir Putin, for example). They didn't get into their positions of power without having an essential ingredient – the ability to influence other people (sell). I'm not saying you intend to run a country – I'm simply making the point that to achieve the very basics in life, you need to be able to sell and close a deal. The better you are at it, the more you'll achieve. Become a master at it, and who knows? Maybe you will run a country (although it doesn't quite fit into the less-stress lifestyle model).

If you don't like selling, or don't class yourself as a good salesperson, I recommend getting some advice on how to sell. Pick up a book (the market is flooded with them), go to a workshop, or speak to people you know who are in sales. Ask them what they believe makes a good salesperson. Here are some of the attributes I think make a top salesperson:

- Persistence and tenacity: A 'never give up' mentality. When others are quitting, you are succeeding.

- Resilience: Being able to take rejection on the chin and quickly bounce back.
- Likeability: People really do buy from people. If people don't like you, you won't sell anything.
- Originality: When everybody else is doing the same thing, you're doing something that sets you apart from the competition.
- Passion: An overused word, but an absolutely essential tool for a top seller. You have to believe in what you do, because if you don't, other people will know it.

Keep time on your side

Time is an interesting subject. On one hand, I believe in grabbing the bull by the horns and that good things come to those who *don't* wait, and on the other, I believe patience can achieve great things – if you have time on your side.

I recently cancelled my gym membership, which had a three-month notice period. A couple of months into the cancellation I realised it was a bad decision, based on other gyms not having the same facilities. I had a bit of time on my side, so I decided to wait before letting the gym know I had changed my mind. Lo and behold, a few weeks before the membership was due to expire I received an email: *We don't want to see you go, Carl, and if you stay we'd like to give you a month free.* This time, time was on my side, and I benefited.

Time can win you a deal and give you massive leverage when negotiating. If somebody needs to sell something quickly, they have no leverage. Think of when you're selling a house. 'The three Ds' (Debt, Divorce and Death) are responsible for a lot of people who are desperate to sell, and desperation will have the vultures circling, ready to pounce. This is a classic example of having to do something because of lack of time.

If you have something to sell, and you want the best price for it, you have to have time on your side. If the situation is desperate, where possible, don't let people know. If you do, you'll find they start growing beaks and wings.

Always aim to keep time on your side and use it to your advantage. Otherwise, it will be used against you.

Be patient(ish)

Sometimes, it pays to be patient. And I speak as somebody who is very impatient. I've always had the attitude: 'if I want something, I'll go and get it'. Sometimes this works, but most of the time it doesn't. It doesn't because I usually get stung. The seller sees the desperation in my eyes, and out comes their stinger.

I've learned that trying to cause a tsunami will only lead to little, short-term success. It's the daily grind and slow chipping away at your goals (the small waves) that make a long-term difference. Again, this is where being patient comes in. As I mentioned, there is a strong argument for 'good things come to those who *don't* wait', so balancing patience, ambition and expectation is a big skill to possess in the game that is life.

> 'True happiness is to enjoy the present, without anxious dependence upon the future, not to amuse ourselves with either hopes or fears but to rest satisfied with what we have, which is sufficient.'
>
> — Seneca, 'The Morals of Seneca: A Selection of his Prose'

The reason I say be patient(ish) is because, unless you're pushing on to bigger and better things, they won't happen. In other words, it's OK to build up to your goal, but you also have to take action to make it happen – to achieve things you never thought you could achieve – otherwise, time will pass you by and you'll live in regret. I'll use my housing situation as an example. When I was living in my two-bed terraced house, paying a very small mortgage, I had very few outgoings and was able to save a good amount of money. Sounding good so far? However, there are two strong arguments for why this is a bad strategy:

1. This two-bed terraced house was my reality (I'm talking my financial comfort zone here). Saving money was nice, but if I wasn't pushing myself to achieve more, I could have quite easily lived in this house for a considerably longer period of time, and I may never have changed my life.
2. It goes against the advice given by Henry Ford, who said that old men are always giving young men bad advice by telling them to save money. Instead, his advice was to invest in yourself; Henry Ford didn't save a dollar until he was forty. In other words, what's the point in saving if you're not making your goals happen by investing in yourself? It's all well and good to make sacrifices in life and have money in the bank, but sometimes you have to ask why you're doing it. If you can utilise your money to invest in yourself to create the lifestyle of your dreams, that's exactly what you should be aiming to do – not living in a house that is smaller than you would like with your money in the bank, earning a pittance in a low-interest savings account.

When I decided to take Henry Ford's advice and change my reality, I moved house and chose to prioritise investing in myself. Now I get to live the lifestyle I want, which pushes me to achieve more, and learn new skills that I know will earn me a lot more than 0.5% interest.

It is important to be grateful for what we have, because concentrating on what we haven't got can cause a lot of unhappiness (because we're always aiming higher). Again, it's about the balance between being grateful and striving for more. It is one of the most difficult balancing acts to perform, but if you can get it right, you're well on your way to a less-stress lifestyle. If you know what you have is enough and it makes you happy without compromising, that's a perfect balance. To strive for more will cause unnecessary stress, and to accept less means you're not fulfilling your potential.

If you want big results, like a bigger house or a better lifestyle, you don't need to create a tsunami. Keep chipping away, safe in the knowledge that the small waves are creating movement. You might get frustrated that you can't see it yet, but it's happening. All the giants had to start somewhere. That first brush stroke on a blank canvas, the first words of a blog on a new website, and that first sales call all lead on to bigger and better things. What you're doing now, including every small action you take, is shaping your success. Sometimes you've just got to be a little patient.

I'd hate to imagine how many fantastic ideas go to waste because the person quit at the vital stage due to a lack of patience. It's a fine line, and if we had the gift of foresight – knowing in advance what would work and what wouldn't – we'd all be much happier and wealthier.

Since we'll never be able to see into the future, we might as well have a bit of fun trying to make our ideas work.

Consider all your actions

How many times have you skipped the gym or eaten that extra piece of cake, promising yourself you'll make up for it, but it never happens? It never happens because it's a state of mind – a routine and a pattern of thinking we get trapped in. Whatever you're doing now is all that counts, not what you're going to do tomorrow.

There's not much point eating junk food continuously for two months because you've promised yourself you'll go on a fast afterwards. It's too late. You've already become unhealthy, potentially developed irreversible health issues, and you'll want more junk food at the end of two months because that's what you've become accustomed to.

A less-stress lifestyle means being consistent and considering *all* your actions and their consequences. It takes huge amounts of discipline, but lying to our future selves is a big reason why we continue in the same situation (or worse). It's why average stays average (or gets worse), and why great gets better. Let me put it this way. If you're unhappy with your life and deem it to be average, are you going to continue doing average things, promising yourself change will happen? Or are you going to develop your disciplinary skills, and actually start making positive changes (now – not tomorrow!)? It's your choice.

Every action you take from this moment forward is dictating your future, no matter what you tell yourself. It doesn't mean you have to live like a saint or banish every vice from your life (life would become very dull, which isn't the aim). You just have to use your common sense and be mindful that consistency is the key to being less stressed.

If you want to predict the future, you only need to take a look at your lifestyle today, and the choices you're making and the actions you're taking (or not). There's no crystal ball required – that is your future.

Chapter 20

Stay happy

The ability to improve your mood is an excellent tool to possess, but the hardest thing to sustain in life is happiness. I'm the first person to admit this. I have to work hard every day to stay happy. Some days it feels like an impossible task, but I know that if I'm trying, I'm having a better day than I would if I wasn't trying.

Accept both the good and bad days

I have lots of days when I just don't feel happy, and I'm OK with that. There is absolutely nothing wrong with having fluctuations in mood – life would be flat without them. In fact, we need the bad days in order to appreciate the good ones!

I've had to work hard to identify the type of lifestyle that works for me, and getting the balance right isn't an easy task. The challenge is making sure you're doing enough to achieve your goals without stressing yourself out. This takes time and practice.

For me to get it right, I need to be challenged with a variety of projects, combined with plenty of relaxation time. If I relax too much, I notice I start to slip into old habits, including procrastination and inaction. If I challenge myself too much and have too much on, I quickly burn out. Burnout for me means getting ill, and being uptight, anxious and short-tempered with my family – these are signs that something isn't right.

Like I say, it's not easy because life is a series of ups and downs. But working hard to get the balance right is key to fulfilling a less-stress lifestyle. Whenever you feel you might be overstretching yourself (or under-stretching), act on it immediately. It might help you to keep a diary of how you feel so you can track it. If you look back at your diary and find that you're spending more than three days feeling stressed, it's time to start paying attention and to do something that you find relaxing – such as booking a spa day, if that's your thing.

It will be harder to identify when you're not pushing yourself enough because it might actually feel good, especially if you've been through periods of high stress. Your body might be craving no stress at all, which is fine, apart from when it starts to affect your future. In other words, if you're not doing anything, you're not making money or helping to create your future. It might feel good now, but it will only lead to more stress (and boredom) in the long run.

Getting the balance right is one of the best skills you can develop, because this will lead to happiness. Keep practising getting it right, and over time you'll have many happier days.

Stay social

At the beginning of the book I mentioned the study conducted by Harvard, which analysed what makes us happy. The key finding from the study was how important social connection is to our happiness. When you have too much time on your hands, you can become socially isolated, so it's important to make an effort to keep a strong social connection with other people.

What do I mean by 'stay social'? I'm not suggesting you start using social media in the hope of vague comments and likes. (I recently read an article in *The Times* called 'One in five depressed by social media' by Rosemary Bennett (see http://www.thetimes.co.uk/article/one-in-five-depressed-by-social-media-9tszbfswr) about research conducted about how depressed social media can make you feel. Figures suggested that about 1 in 5 adults in the UK got depressed when they saw their connections on social media having a good time when they weren't. It's a bit of a no-brainer, really. Of course you're going to get fed up if you see your friend having a ball on holiday in Australia when you're stuck in the office, chained to your desk!)

This was further backed up when I heard a psychologist talking about social media on my local BBC radio station. She said that many people write posts only to get likes, rather than for personal joy. It's hard to imagine the satisfaction in that. Where is the substance? Who cares about virtual 'likes' if you have real-life friends to go out with?

I don't have a personal Facebook account, yet I still manage to meet up with friends. I certainly don't feel as though I'm missing anything. In fact, if I compare myself to some of my friends who are addicted to Facebook, I'd say not having an account means I'm more active and physically do more things than they do.

However, I can understand the addiction. Assuming most people are as nosey as I am, knowing what's going on in other people's lives can quickly become addictive. Online game companies have got wise to this by creating games that punish you if you take a day off playing: in FarmVille, your animals and crops will die if you don't feed them each day.

It's hard to avoid social media, seeing as it's everywhere and so many people use it, but it isn't the only way to connect with people. Sometimes a good old-fashioned call to a friend is just what the doctor ordered. If you feel yourself becoming addicted to social media (let's define addicted: if I asked you to stop using social media for a day, would you struggle?), slowly wean yourself off it. If, for example, part of your routine is checking your Facebook page at lunchtime, don't do it. Do something else, like have a conversation with a colleague at work. I question anybody who says they are happier sitting in front of a computer looking at pictures of people at a party, rather than actually being at the party themselves.

Take the time to get out of the house and away from your computer screen. Go out and live life, and stay social. It's proven – good relationships will keep you fit, free, healthy and happy.

Take responsibility

Picking fault and finding reasons for not liking people is easy – much easier than making the effort to stay social. It's also easy to not take responsibility for your own actions.

There were periods of my life when I became very bitter towards others, and I blamed them for me feeling so awful. I was looking at it completely wrong. The reality was, I was feeling sorry for myself. In my highly anxious and stressed state of mind, it was easier for me to stay at home blaming everybody else for the way I felt than it was for me to do anything about it. It was only when I understood that I was in complete control of how others made me feel that I started to embrace them. Knowing I held this power meant I could develop friendships and relationships based on trust, without a hidden agenda.

You're only going to find happiness and peace within yourself when you don't allow anybody else to dictate or control your emotions.

It was up to me how somebody else's words made me feel. I could choose to take what they said with a pinch of salt, or I could continuously replay their words in my mind until I couldn't take any more, and therefore avoided any further hurt by removing people from my life.

There are over seven billion people on the planet. Like it or loathe it, social interaction is a fundamental part of any healthy lifestyle. You don't need to become the socialite of the century, but it's important to feel comfortable around others. A good start is to stop finding fault and criticising others, and instead learn to understand and accept people for who they are. Hate and bitterness will eat you up inside, and knock your balance completely out of sync. Love, empathy and acceptance will help you grow, and significantly reduce your stress.

Another priority, before you learn to love and accept others, is learning to look in the mirror and love what you see. You can't do one without the other.

'I don't deserve to be happy.'
'I can't break this crippling stress.'
'My life will never change.'

These are just a few of the thoughts I used to beat myself up with every day. I would look in the mirror and really dislike the person looking back. I used to wonder how I'd let my life get so bad, and blame myself for it. Why would anybody want me around them?

If these sound familiar, remember that you owe it to yourself to achieve what you want in life. You *do* deserve to be happy, and you *can* break the pattern. Your life will change if you want it to. You are just as special and deserving as anybody else on this planet. Love yourself – you have a lot to offer.

Fill your time

The purpose of this book is to teach you how to live in a way that will give you more free time. Let's say you've done that (I'm proud of you!). Now, it's time to fill that time. There's no pressure, of course, but I'm assuming you haven't worked hard to create more time to just sit at home all day? If you have, and that makes you happy, that's fine. However, I know that too much idle time can become unconstructive and can sometimes lead to being depressed – just as depressed as you were when you rushed around all day and had to time to rest.

It's time to get a new game plan. We have to prevent any further potential negativity (including procrastination and self-doubt) by filling your time. But there's a big difference: now *you* dictate what, where, when and how you want to do something, rather it being dictated by somebody else.

If you ever feel that you're getting bored or stuck, or that you have too much time on your hands, I'd like you to revisit Action 4: Focus. It will make sure you're on the right track by having a focus and setting goals for yourself. Whenever you feel bored or stuck, it's because your focus is off.

It's also worth noting that you can have too much of a good thing. Those cocktails at the start of your holiday don't taste as sweet a couple of weeks into the holiday, do they? It's human nature to want what we can't have, and not to be fussed about the things we know we can have. This is why I'm not keen on becoming so wealthy that I don't know what to do with all my money. When you know you can have anything you want at any time, where's the fun – the chase?

Although we don't always appreciate it, especially when we're at rock bottom, feeling as though we're constantly chasing the dollar, the chase is part of the fun. Use it, and always appreciate it. 'The chase' doesn't have to refer to making money. The chase could apply to a new relationship, a new charity, or a new you. The options are endless. Fill your time, continue to grow, and don't stagnate (physically or mentally).

Be grateful

The biggest and best tool I can give you to stay happy is gratitude. Gratitude will instantly destroy any negative thoughts – something stress feeds off. If you're grateful for everything you have, and not fearful of the things you don't have, it's impossible to allow stress to dominate your mind.

Why do dock leaves grow near stinging nettles? Nature always wants to provide us with a solution. **Gratitude is nature's solution to stress**. If you feel grateful every day, your outlook on life will completely change.

Does being grateful mean I shouldn't have ambition or want more out of life?

Not at all, no. Again, it's about getting the balance right. As I mentioned previously, there is a fine line between being grateful for what we have and wanting more in life. Distinguishing between the two is important.

For example, if you're a multi-millionaire and your goal in life is to keep doubling your money each year, but this goal keeps you in a highly stressed state of mind, why are you doing it? Have you sat down and really thought about why you're doing what you're doing? I've used this example specifically because I've met people who have amassed great fortunes, only to keep running themselves into the ground by working harder than ever before. They've made a million, so now they must make two, or three, or ten. They throw happiness out of the window for the sake of achieving a goal. I understand that their fear of losing their money is probably the driving force behind their actions, but it pays to regularly evaluate our goals and check to see they're still a good fit for us.

Some people have very little money and material possessions, yet they're grateful for *something* in their lives. They're not eaten up inside with resentment and jealousy. They have very little but they still help others, without giving a second thought to what they don't have or should get in return. Are these people closer to knowing what life is really about? I don't know. What I do know is, if a goal is making you unhappy, you should stop striving for it, especially if you don't need to. Strive to achieve goals that make you happy. Help other people when you can, no matter your current situation, and be grateful for what you have.

There is a TEDx talk by Louie Schwartzberg called 'Gratitude' (find it on YouTube) that sums up gratitude brilliantly. You can also find it on my blog on my website at http://www.carlvernon.com/blog/gratitude-the-anxiety-killer.

Chapter 21

Keep taking action

Now you should have a better understanding of what you have to do, and the tools you need to create a less-stress lifestyle. So, what next? Good question. Actually, it's a fabulous question, because this bit makes *all* the difference!

There is a massive difference between being a doer and a talker. I meet a lot of talkers and very few doers. If anybody ever asks me how I've achieved the things I have, I always say it's because I'm a doer rather than a talker. I start writing the book rather than talk about writing it. I buy the investment property rather than think about buying it. I make the sales call rather than wonder how winning the client could improve my revenue. My actions aren't always accurate, and they don't always work, but taking action (whether it works or not) is always better than not taking action at all.

I've always been intrigued by why we don't do things we know could lead us to great things, even if they are tiny actions. I'm speaking very much from a personal viewpoint here. Although I've given examples of actions

I've taken above, there were many periods of my life when I procrastinated. It was always down to one thing: **inaction**.

The only thing that separates great from average is action. The only reason you won't achieve your goals is if you don't take action – it really is that simple.

The reason I meet so many talkers is because it's easier to talk about something rather than it is to do it. Or is it? If you analyse your goal, the small action you need to take to get the ball rolling rarely takes strenuous effort. It's certainly no harder to spend the evening talking about your great idea rather than put the wheels in motion to actually make it happen. It's self-doubt and fear of rejection that puts people off taking action.

So, how do you become a doer and stop being a talker? Most of the answer to this question has been covered in the book, but here's a very quick answer: **Start taking action, and don't ever stop taking action!**

> 'Be about actions, not distractions.'
>
> — Unknown

Action doesn't need to be extravagant to start with – you just need to make a start. Small steps lead to big results. Make a plan and take it step by step. For now, forget about the end result or objective. If the end goal is your focus, you probably won't start the process. You'll remind yourself of how much hard work there is to be done, and how it's never going to happen anyway.

Too many of us focus on the specifics – the 'this is why it's not going to happen'. This will only allow self-doubt and procrastination to take over. The things that make the real difference come from the action of starting something. Deciding to get on the plane makes the real difference, rather than the journey itself. You just have to decide to get on the plane and the rest will follow. Just focus on the next small step, get it done, and then move on to the next small step. Before you know it, you'll be at the end of the yellow brick road.

The only thing you need to be sure of is that you want what you've set out to achieve. This is where thinking time and planning are valuable. Developing your action-taking skills is great, but if you keep going after things you realise you don't want, you will eventually become disillusioned and demotivated, resulting in future inaction.

Get a 'results buddy'

Your 'have tos' and self-motivation can only go so far. If you want consistent results, you're going to need a results buddy. *A results buddy?* I hear you ask. Let me explain . . .

Even the most self-driven individual will need support eventually. This is why coaches exist – sometimes we need that extra push, support and guidance. A coach will help you take responsibility for your actions and results, which makes your chances of success much greater, compared to relying solely on yourself. And that's where a results buddy comes in – he will help and support you with your goals, like a coach.

Having a results buddy is also positive, because we don't want to let people down. If you tell somebody you're going to do something, you're much more likely to do it. You don't want to look like a fool or a time-waster, and if you've told somebody you're going to do something, you'll get it done.

Humans need approval from others. *If I don't do that, he's going to think I'm a loser. If I tell her I'm going to do that I'd better go through with it.* Your need for approval from your results buddy is going to help you achieve things you never thought possible – things you might struggle with if you depended solely on your own motivation. Group meetings (such as Alcoholics Anonymous or stop smoking groups) are effective for this exact reason.

A results buddy can be a friend, mentor, family member, colleague or pretty much anybody you have respect for. Respect is essential because you need to be able to listen to them and take on board what they say. More importantly, it has to be important to you that you don't let them down.

An even better scenario is if you can return the favour, and you also act as their results buddy. You'll both be working towards goals (maybe similar/same goals), and there will be extra motivation from both sides – maybe even a little healthy competition! Your results buddy doesn't need to be an expert in the field of your goal(s); they just need to have common sense, and the ability to help you look at things a little differently if and when needed.

Think who you'd like as your results buddy. Then call them and say:

> Hi.
>
> Listen, I need your help [most people will want to help you].
>
> I have this goal I'm looking to achieve [explain what the goal is], and I'd like you to be my results buddy [briefly explain what a results buddy is].
>
> I'm going to tell you exactly what my plan is, and exactly when I'm looking to achieve each step. I'll call you at each step to let you know I've done it, and if I haven't, I'll tell you why.

> If you don't feel I'm working to my full potential, or if I'm making excuses, I'd like you to tell me and I'll always take on board your advice and feedback – and, more importantly, act on it.
>
> Because you're doing this for me, what goal can I help you achieve, so we can work together to make sure it happens?

Make the call today.

Use your blueprint

Once you have a blueprint for something that works for you, there will be no stopping you. You'll be able to adapt this success strategy to anything that takes your fancy, and your path will be lined with gold.

I'm sure you've met one of those annoying people who seems to be good at everything, right? This is no coincidence. They understand what works for them. They have a blueprint for success and adapt it to whatever they do in life. If it works for one thing, it works for something else. (Qualities are completely transferable, whatever you do.)

You've probably also heard of millionaires who have gained and lost their fortunes many times over. Again, this is down to having a blueprint for making money.

They know what it takes to make millions, and they repeat what worked for them previously. The reason the cycle continues is because they also repeat their overspending each time they make a million.

My blueprint is very much what you've read in this book. Sticking to the principles in this book helps me succeed in whatever I do. I have no doubt they will do the same for you, as long as you're adopting them around who you are. In other words, continue to be true to yourself by doing what makes you feel comfortable and feels right for you.

The sooner you start drawing, and using, your blueprint the better. The pencil in your hand is ready for your ideas, and the drawing starts when you start taking action (remember, small steps). Most pencils come with an eraser for a reason. Sometimes you'll need to take a step back, refocus, or even start again. It's well worth the effort, though, because once your blueprint is in place, it's there for good.

Like any blueprint, it can be tweaked, modernised and updated, but the basis of the drawing will always remain. This is your key to all future success. You'll know when you have a good one in place because it will work. If it doesn't, grab your eraser and start again.

Staying less stressed

I've mentioned on more than one occasion in this book that I don't have a very high tolerance level to stress. Because of this, sometimes I fall into my bad old habits and find myself dealing with higher than normal levels of stress.

I have to evaluate my life on a regular basis and remind myself to take a break when required. It's not easy; life has a way of pulling me back into its highly pressured and stressful grasp. We're all under pressure to achieve a certain level in life (in the form of money, material objects or success), whatever our situation. This pressure comes from both other people and ourselves. It's this type of pressure that can very quickly pull us back into the type of life you've been learning to avoid throughout this book.

Achieving a less-stress lifestyle takes continuous effort and evaluation. How often you do this is up to you. I have to review my lifestyle at least once a week to make sure I'm sticking to my principles. It's not easy going against the status quo and having people around you telling you what and how you should be doing something, and that you must be crazy for not getting a steady job with a large company. You have to be dedicated and committed to changing your life. It's hard work, but the rewards are worth it!

Evaluate and refocus however often you need to, and when you feel yourself slipping back into your old life, bring your stress levels back down by adopting the things you've learned in this book.

No excuses

Some people are born into money. Some people get a head start in life because they receive a large inheritance. Some people will look as though success naturally gravitates towards them, and happiness just falls at their feet. There will always be people more physically and mentally able than you. You can guarantee all these things – but you can also be sure that there is always somebody less able than you who will achieve great things.

It's all well and good having a lottery win, but it's what you do with it that really counts. There are countless examples of individuals who have squandered such gifts. Why? Who knows? What is always evident is a lack of passion and desire. I would back somebody who is broke but who has passion and desire over an unmotivated, lacklustre lottery-winner any day of the week.

Yes, it's nice to have a head start, whether in the form of money or doting parents, but it won't decide your fate. If you have passion, you can accomplish anything you set out to do – and we all have access to bags of it.

As soon as you start to say things like, 'Yeah, but he had this', or 'She was given that', you'll start to slide down a slippery slope of underachievement, destined always to live in the world of *that never happened for me because . . .*

Don't let that happen! There is no 'because'. You create your own opportunities; never forget that. There are no excuses. If you don't go out and create your own opportunities, that's completely down to you, nobody else. It's not up to your parents, partner, friends or family. Nobody else is going to take responsibility for your life if you don't.

Forget about what you have – and don't have. Stop comparing yourself to others. If you have the passion and desire, you will make things happen. Excuses will no longer exist. Holding on to negative thoughts will hold you – and your true potential – back.

Still afraid of change?

Being afraid of change will keep you trapped in the same thoughts, routine and lifestyle.

'I won't be able to pay the bills.'
'My career will be ruined.'
'If I fail, I'll never be able to turn it around.'

All of these common lies we tell ourselves are misconceptions that prevent us from growing. They are the brick walls that stand between us and a less-stress lifestyle. The only difference between people who go for their dreams and people who stay rooted in fear is the belief that these walls can be knocked down. The truth is, the walls *can* be knocked down – you were built to survive, whatever your situation. As long as you act smart you will always be able to pay the bills, your career won't be ruined, and you can turn any situation around. How do I know this? Because you *have to*. (Remember your 'have tos'?)

My intention in this book is to open your mind and help you look at things differently. I know how difficult it is to try something new. I know how challenging it is to change. I want to stress here again: whether you decide to keep your day job, start a new venture, or go and live in the hills, I just want you to be aware that having more happiness and less stress is absolutely possible, even by making relatively small changes to your life.

Don't be afraid to fail. It's the only way you're going to learn. Look at everything you do as an opportunity to learn, and appreciate that sometimes it might not go according to plan. All the top achievers have failed countless times. I know I've failed more times than I've succeeded, but you'll find that the times you succeed make more of a difference. This is another reason you shouldn't fear failure – it is temporary, and you can bounce back from anything.

I'm placing emphasis on failing, not to scare or discourage you, but because it will happen to you if you're going to reach the life you want. I could have quit years ago, and on many occasions I nearly did. After years of frustration and constant disappointment, I almost decided to throw in the towel. The reason I'm living my less-stress lifestyle today, though, is that I didn't quit.

No regrets

A common deathbed regret is that we worked too hard. If you aim for a less-stress lifestyle, you can change this today. This doesn't have to be you.

I don't have a magic answer for you, but my advice is never to stop reaching for the things you want in life. Never stop following what you really want.

How badly do you want it? Does it scare you that your life might not change? Does it frighten you to think you might never fulfil your potential? If you're more scared of not taking the chance than you are about continuing to stay as you are, you'll take the chance. Our biggest fears drive us, so let the fear of not trying drive you. Make it so you *have to* start.

If you envisage living a less-stress life and *believe* it will happen, it will. You just have to decide to be whoever you want to be from this day forward, and you will become that person.

This life is your one shot to make a difference. Don't waste it. Take a chance.

A less-stress lifestyle is waiting for you, and all you need to do is start.

Action is the game-changer

- Start being true to yourself – today.
- Start investing in yourself – today.
- Start using perception to boost and improve your mood – today.
- Start looking at your environment and decide who, and what, is going to help move your life forward – today.
- Start dropping the negative emotional attachments you don't need – today.
- Start looking at SAO – today.
- Start making money work for you and put things in place that will generate a passive income – today.
- Start being grateful for what you have, rather than complain about what you don't have – today.
- Stop making excuses – today.
- Start taking action, today, and never stop taking action.

Good things come to those who *don't* wait.

Let's continue your journey . . .

I'd like to help you continue your journey to a less-stress lifestyle, and on my website you'll find more: www.carlvernon.com

Sign up for my free updates, a workshop or an event, check out my blog, drop me a line on social media – whatever takes your fancy.

I look forward to hearing about your less-stress lifestyle success story.

Best wishes,

Carl Vernon

Acknowledgements

Thanks go out to my editor Jane Hammett for another outstanding piece of work. To my agent Jen Christie, for your support throughout. To Muna Reyal and Kate Miles at Headline for making it happen. And to my family and friends for your constant inspiration.

Index